The
CATHEDRALS
of the British Isles

EXCALIBUR ✠ BOOKS

Published in the United States by
Excalibur Books, 201 Park Avenue South,
New York, NY 10003.

Not to be sold outside of USA and
its territories

© Marshall Cavendish Limited 1978

Printed in Great Britain

ISBN 0 525 70261 X

Contents

CATHEDRALS:
an introduction

Today Britain's cathedrals are regarded as much as architectural treasure houses as places of worship. Standing as a lasting memorial and tribute to the skills of a bygone age, they have become part of our cultural heritage, something to be nurtured and well cared for. Yet, it was not always so. The eighteenth and nineteenth centuries saw a spate of restoration, an excess of zeal, with not necessarily pleasing results. James Wyatt, the eighteenth century architect, so drastically 'restored' the work of earlier craftsmen that he was considered later to have done more harm than the efforts of Henry VIII's Dissolution and the Puritan vandals combined.

The mid-nineteenth century, however, saw the arrival of Sir George Gilbert Scott, the most renowned architect of his day. He is probably best remembered for designing the Albert Memorial in London's Hyde Park, but his work on nearly half of the country's cathedrals is of far more importance. Scott gave them a new lease of life. True, there was the occasional stylistic lapse but on the whole he not only managed to undo as much as he could of Wyatt's folly, but also ensured that his own restoration was a genuine attempt to give the cathedral back its former glory.

Most people equate cathedrals with size; they think of York's massiveness or Salisbury's soaring spire, but sheer bulk has nothing to do with it. Quite simply, a cathedral is no more than a church which contains the throne of a bishop. The word itself is derived from the Greek *cathedra*, meaning chair. The cathedral became the centre of the diocese, or area over which its bishop had religious jurisdiction.

Until 1535 all the cathedrals, as well as monasteries and churches, were Roman

Below: A typical cathedral built and altered over several centuries. Although not based on any particular cathedral, all the features shown might be found together in the same building. The west front and nave are in the Romanesque style, with round arches, massive walls and small windows. This flourished in England in the 11th century, but had been established in Europe for some centuries previously. The transepts, tower and choir are 'Early English', the first English Gothic style, lighter with pointed arches and tall, narrow 'lancet' windows. East of the altar, the building is Perpendicular, a style not found on the Continent, distinguished by its straight lines.

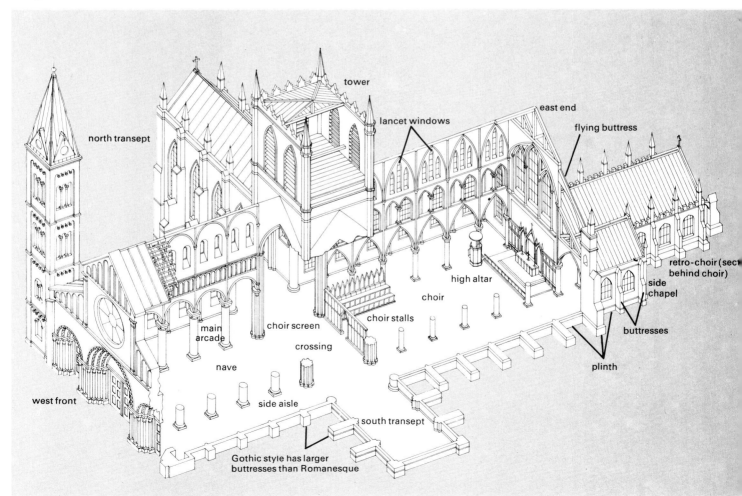

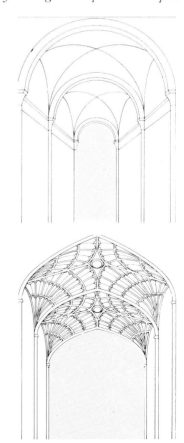

Catholic, ruled by the Pope in Rome. The early sixteenth century, however, saw a swelling discontent with the way the church conducted its affairs, seemingly increasing its wealth at the expense of the populace and at the same time blithely disregarding their welfare, spiritual or temporal.

It was in Germany that Martin Luther spearheaded the break with Rome and the impetus soon spread throughout Europe. In England in particular, there was a growth in the new Protestant religion especially among the young intelligentsia. These included men like Tyndale and Coverdale, who translated the Bible into English, Latimer and Cranmer, later to become Henry VIII's Archbishop of Canterbury.

It was against this setting that the English Reformation took place. In order to marry Anne Boleyn Henry VIII demanded that Pope Clement VII should annul his marriage to Catherine of Aragon stating that as Catherine had previously been married to his late brother, Arthur, the marriage was invalid. The Pope refused. As a virtual prisoner of Charles V, the powerful Holy Roman Emperor and Catherine's nephew, he had no choice.

This apparent Papal obduracy gave Henry the excuse he needed. He was well aware of the influences at work in Rome and bitterly resented being subject to the whims of foreign potentates. Over the next five years he gradually cut England off from the Catholic Church in Rome. He declared himself, through Parliament, Supreme Head of the Church of England, stripped the clergy of its power and privilege and dissolved the monasteries.

The Religious Reformation marked the end of one era for the church and the start of another. Henry seized abbey lands and sold them; church interiors were wrecked and most of the precious items removed to the royal coffers. Many of the buildings were destroyed, either merely for the sake of destruction or to provide stone for some secular purpose: Oxford Cathedral is a case in point; it was partially demolished by Cardinal Wolsey so that he could build what was later to become Christ Church College.

Once it was recognized that the Church was now truly subservient to the State, no more building of any importance occurred until St Paul's in the late seventeenth century. There was a flurry of activity in the eighteenth and nine-

Below: Two forms of vault found in cathedrals. The first, a groined vault, a development of the simple Romanesque barrel vault. The second, the fan vault, characteristic of the English Perpendicular style.

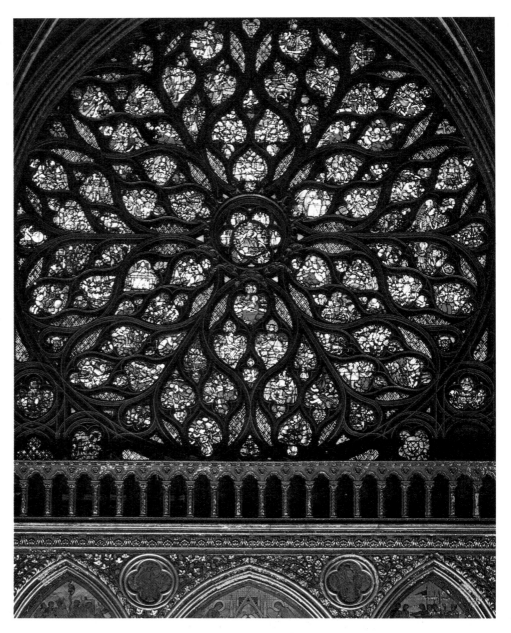

teenth centuries but this was as much a restoration of the old as it was the creation of anything new.

The mid-seventeenth century witnessed England's Civil War and yet another setback to the great cathedrals and churches. Cromwell's soldiers stabled their horses in the naves, smashed irreplaceable medieval stained glass, tore down statues, wrecked fine old carving and generally caused as much wanton destruction as they could. The cathedral exteriors were, for the most part, spared the indignity of cannon bombardment but, nevertheless, it took the majority of them almost two centuries to recover.

This was as long as some of them had taken to build. The earliest cathedrals, dating from the Anglo-Saxon period, were usually built of timber or in very basic stone. Very few traces of these survive most having been burnt down, devastated by raids or demolished by the Normans.

The Normans were the first to build cathedrals in the grand manner. William the Conqueror replaced virtually all the Anglo-Saxon bishops and appointed his own from Normandy. Each one wanted his own distinctive cathedral, something that would preserve its builder's name for posterity.

Norman architecture, also known as *Romanesque* because of its tendency to follow the Roman pattern, lasted until around 1150. It is characterized by bulk: heavy pillars, thick walls and sturdy semi-circular arches. The design is that of a Latin cross formed by a nave and transepts. There is usually a low, square central tower or twin towers at the west end. Stone vaulting would be used only over fairly narrow stretches and decoration tended to be fanciful and bold.

By the mid-twelfth century *Romanesque* architecture was giving way to *Early English Gothic*. Arches became pointed and pillars tall and slender with stone vaults covering wider sections of the roof. It was all a great improvement on the solidity of the Normans but still lacked overall finesse which followed in the next important development, *Decorated Gothic*. It was an architectural flowering, growing stronger from 1250 to 1350. Design became much more elaborate; parapets and pinnacles appeared, doorways were less recessed, windows were enlarged and given tracery of geometric precision, the nave was usually widened and, above all, the cathedral was filled with exquisite carving.

This was followed by the more straightforward *Perpendicular Gothic*. This developed in the mid-fourteenth century and lasted until about 1540. The Black Death of 1348 had wiped out almost half the population, including the craftsmen engaged in cathedral building and decoration. As a result cathedrals became lighter places. The walls were not so thick, columns were slender, windows were larger, and the emphasis was placed on light, space and a new refined delicacy.

Henry VIII and Cromwell effectively dampened any architectural enthusiasm during the sixteenth and seventeenth centuries and it was 1675 before the foundation stone of St Paul's, England's only cathedral built during this period, was laid. Sir Christopher Wren's masterpiece is built in the *Renaissance* style, the first and last major cathedral of its kind in Britain.

The return to Gothic architecture of the eighteenth and nineteenth centuries both in new building and the restoration of the old has been surpassed by the twentieth century cathedrals. They have no form dictated by time: they can be as traditional as the great Anglican cathedral in Liverpool or as adventurous as Coventry.

Below left: An illustration from a 15th century French bible showing Solomon watching the building of the Temple. It is, in fact, a building of the period, and the picture shows contemporary workers scribing a stone before cutting it to shape, carrying roofing materials up a ladder, hammering roofing lead into place and, in the background, mixing mortar with a wooden shovel.

Below: York Minster was built without proper foundations, being simply supported on thousands of wooden piles driven into the soil. When these started to give way, the only solution was to replace them with modern concrete, but the task was complicated by having to work entirely from underneath to avoid disturbing the fabric.

Armagh
St Patrick's Church of Ireland Cathedral

Armagh is the ecclesiastical capital of Ireland, being the seat of both the Archbishop of the Church of Ireland and that of the Roman Catholic church. Each faith has its own cathedral, each confusingly called St Patrick's

The history of St Patrick's Church of Ireland Cathedral dates back to the fifth century when it was founded by the saint himself. By the ninth century the building was known locally as 'the great stone church'. However in 1268 the incumbent Primate began an extensive remodelling which eventually absorbed all traces of the earlier work except the arches of the crypt. The existing transepts date from this period. In the mid-fourteenth century St Patrick's was extended further, serving 200 years later as a fortress during an uprising against Elizabeth I. Consequently the cathedral was badly damaged and left a ruin until 1613 when another restoration was started.

St Patrick's is fairly small, just 182 feet long, and is unusual in that the nave and

Below: The original church of St Patrick, founded in the fifth century, has long since disappeared. However, his name has been preserved and the cathedral which occupies the same site today stands as a pleasing tribute to his memory.

Left: The north aisle contains some fine pieces of statuary including the recumbent figure of Dean Drelincourt by Michael Rysbrack, the Flemish sculptor.

choir do not align. This is believed to symbolize the attitude of Christ's head on the cross.

The cathedral houses some fine statues including, in the nave, an eighteenth-century study of Sir Thomas Molyneux by the noted sculptor, Louis Roubillac. There is also a remarkable recumbent effigy of the Dean Drelincourt, sculptured by the Flemish Michael Rysbrack. The moulding on the great west door incorporates an intriguing collection of pagan carvings while high up on the cathedral's exterior walls there is a splendid assortment of medieval carvings.

The Chapter House contains several mysterious stone statues, one of which is thought to be Queen Macha, while the library houses a selection of rare books and manuscripts. The most interesting of these was written in Italian by a fourteenth-century monk, Brother Stephanus, who claimed that is was dictated to him in colloquial Italian by St Catherine of Sienna when he was in a trance. There is also a copy of Gulliver's Travels with corrections by Swift.

Bristol

Bristol is unique in that it is the only English example of what the Germans define as a hall church, that is a church in which the nave, choir and aisles are the same height.

It was founded as an Augustinian monastery in 1140 and consecrated in 1165. Parts of the original building still survive, most notably the Chapter House. Approached through a delightfully dignified Romanesque vestibule this is generally regarded as one of the finest Norman rooms in the country with its remarkable zigzag moulding and interwoven arches lending a special quality.

Another of Bristol's unique features is the fact that it possesses two Lady Chapels. The first of these, the Elder Lady Chapel, was built in 1215 and is situated off the choir's north aisle. It contains a great deal of rich carving on the capitals of the pillars and between the shoulders of the arches. The craftsmen who executed the exquisite detail were on secondment from the great West Country cathedral at Wells.

The Eastern Lady Chapel, conventionally sited beyond the High Altar, followed in the early fourteenth century at the same time as the choir. It too is finely decorated and boasts the first lierne vault in England. The medieval colours of the reredos behind the altar have been carefully restored and it seems to glow with light and warmth. Lining the walls are the tombs of various abbots including that of Abbot Newbury (1428–1473), whose tomb rests in an ornate stellate recess, and the rather bizarre sixteenth-century cadaver tomb of Bristol's first bishop, Paul Bush.

The choir shares the same magnificent lierne vault as the Eastern Lady Chapel and has the tallest arches in England. The aisles feature probably the most splendid stellate recesses in the country as well as an intriguing vault crossed with stone bridges, each bearing three carved heads. Just off the south choir aisle is the sacristy with its elegant roof and the early fourteenth century Berkeley Chapel. This contains the unusual tomb chest of Thomas, Lord Berkeley and his wife. Hanging from the ceiling is a delicately worked medieval candelabrum. It was made in 1460 and is the oldest of its kind in any English church.

Right: This exquisite candelabrum was made in 1460 and is believed to be the oldest of its kind in any English church. It depicts St George slaying the dragon and is surmounted by a figure of the Madonna and Child.

Opposite: Bristol Cathedral's 19th-century west front with its twin towers. One of them contains a peal of bells rescued from Temple Church, Bristol when it was destroyed by bombs in 1940.

Overleaf: The High Altar backed by the intricately carved reredos.

Canterbury

Canterbury, mother church of the Anglican faith and scene of the martyrdom of Thomas Becket, is one of Britain's best known and most visited cathedrals.

Its first stones were laid in 597 when Augustine arrived from Rome with a party of monks to baptize King Ethelbert of Kent. Augustine's cathedral – a simple oblong building with an apse at each end and north and south towers – survived until 1067 when it was gutted by fire.

Undaunted, the first Norman archbishop, Lanfranc, lately Abbot of Caen, began the task of rebuilding. Within a surprisingly short time – seven years – Canterbury once more had a cathedral. It had a central tower, a nave, transepts and twin towers with pinnacles of gold. But in 1174, four years after Canterbury's most famous incumbent, Thomas Becket had been struck down following an injudicious remark by Henry II, windblown sparks and ashes caught between the lead roof and the joists: the lead melted and the building went up in great gusts of flame. Only the nave survived.

Rebuilding took ten years. It was started by a Frenchman, William of Sens, and completed by an English master-mason after William was crippled by a fall. Their most important commission was re-siting the shrine of the now canonized Thomas Becket. This was done by first restoring and then extending the eastern choir. In 1200, amidst a great deal of pomp and ceremony, the saint's remains were

Below: The cathedral from the south west. The porch forms the main entrance for daily use.

Above: The cloister at Canterbury, a fine example of perpendicular lierne vaulting with heraldic bosses commemorating donors to the cathedral's reconstruction.

Right: The exterior of Canterbury Cathedral presents a wide variety of styles which perhaps have little unity but each with its own inherent beauty.

Far right: Canterbury's stained glass is among some of the most remarkable in the world. This thirteenth century window portrays the parable of the rich man.

brought up from the crypt and placed in their new resting place – Trinity Chapel – where they were later joined by the magnificent tombs of the Black Prince and Henry IV.

Becket's sumptuous jewel encrusted shrine was to prove one of the cathedral's greatest attractions for the next 350 years as pilgrims poured in from all over the world. But in 1538 Henry VIII declared the saint a rebel and a traitor: his shrine was desecrated and its treasure appropriated for the royal coffers.

Towards the end of the fourteenth century the Norman nave had deteriorated to such an extent that it was pulled down and rebuilt in the early Perpendicular style. It is set at a slight angle to the choir. The great central bell with its exquisite fan vaulted lantern is one of the finest examples of its kind. It is known as Bell Harry – and was built at the end of the fifteenth century in place of the original

Below: Looking east along the splendidly proportioned and graceful nave. Completed in 1410 under the direction of Henry Yevele, Henry IV's master mason, it replaced the earlier and much deteriorated Norman nave.

Above: The choir at Canterbury. Much of the original was destroyed following a fire in 1174 and was restored to its present glory twenty five years later.

Left: The tomb of Canterbury's most famous Archbishop, St Thomas Becket, cruelly murdered by four knights under the illusion that it was the wish of Henry II. An elaborate tomb was erected in his memory, in time becoming a major focal point for pilgrims. However, it was desecrated under the orders of Henry VIII in 1538 and this simple tomb now stands on the site of the original shrine.

Angel Steeple. Bell Harry, so named because it once housed a single bell called Harry, has been described as 'the queenliest tower in Christendom'.

Apart from the splendour of the architecture, the tombs, chapels, cloisters and painted panels, Canterbury's most impressive feature is its twelfth and thirteenth century stained glass, undoubtedly the loveliest in Britain. Other outstanding features include the early fifteenth century carved stone pulpitum which separates the choir from the nave; the ancient marble throne of the archbishops, believed to date from 1210; the tomb of Henry Chichele, archbishop from 1414 to 1443 – depicting him both in his splendid vestments and as a wasted naked corpse – and, of course, the Martyrdom where Thomas Becket fell under the swords of Henry II's avenging knights.

Chester

A tenth century Anglo-Saxon church, built to house the relics of St Werburgh, the abbess daughter of a Mercian king, once stood on the site of Chester Cathedral. This gave way to a Norman Benedictine Abbey which was itself rebuilt between the thirteenth and sixteenth centuries.

The first building to be completed was the Lady Chapel. Much of it was restored by Sir Gilbert Scott in the nineteenth century while some of the fittings are even later. At the back stands the sadly mutilated shrine of St Werburgh. It dates from about 1310 and until 1876 it formed part of the Bishop's Throne in the choir.

After the Lady Chapel came the choir. It was built by Richard of Chester, one of Edward I's military engineers in Wales, and contains probably Chester's finest feature, the exquisitely carved stalls. The misericords, small carvings under ledges on which to lean during services, are particularly notable and surpass those in most British cathedrals. The gates to the north and south aisles of the choir are made of sixteenth century Spanish wrought-iron. However, the screen which separates the choir from the nave is a Victorian replacement of one from the Middle Ages.

The nave itself was completed in the sixteenth century and is a mixture of

Left: Standing on the site of an ancient Saxon church, the much restored Chester Cathedral retains much of its dignity.

Below: The 14th century choir stalls feature some of the finest carved medieval misericords in Britain.

Above: The richly carved and decorated 14th century choir stalls are separated from the nave by a 19th century screen.

Decorated and late-Perpendicular styles. At the west end of the south aisle, in an unfinished Norman tower, is the nineteenth century baptistry. The font, also of the same period, is Venetian. On the other side of the nave, in the base of the unfinished south tower, is the seventeenth century consistory court. The court, with its oak table and screens, was presided over by the Chancellor of the diocese and was used for trying ecclesiastical offences. It is the only example of such a court left anywhere in the country.

Much of Chester was restored in the nineteenth century – not always harmoniously – but the monks' domestic buildings remain almost as they were in the Middle Ages. These are the best preserved monastic buildings in Britain and give a very good idea of what life was like. They are grouped around the cloister on the north side of the cathedral and include the splendid thirteenth century monks' dining hall or refectory. At one end is the stone dais used by the abbot and important visitors.

The oldest surviving part of Chester is a sturdy eleventh century arch and arcade in the north transept, leading from a chapel into the sacristy. Another interesting feature is the thirteenth century chapter house in the Early English style. Its entrance vestibule is particularly charming.

Chichester

The tapering graceful spire of Chichester Cathedral stands as a landmark for miles around. It soars 277 feet into the sky, dominating the west Sussex countryside and the picturesque city below.

Chichester was built towards the end of the eleventh century on the site of an older collegiate church. In 1114 a fire devastated much of the work but builders repaired the damage and by 1184 the cathedral was virtually finished. Three years later another fire broke out, severely damaging the eastern end. Again it was repaired but this time a stone vault was added and extensive alterations were made to the retrochoir. The two bays behind the high altar were completely remodelled in the Transitional style – the period between Norman and Gothic. The result, an impressive combination of Norman severity and Gothic charm, is one of Chichester's outstanding features.

The retrochoir used to contain the shrine of St Richard, canonized in 1262 and thereafter the focus of pilgrims' devotions for 300 years until Henry VIII ordered its destruction.

The addition of chapels to either side of the nave in the thirteenth century made Chichester – with its corresponding double aisles – the third widest cathedral in England. The upper stage of the central tower with its plate-tracery windows also belongs to this period. The spire, rising from the central tower,

Below: The Arundel Tomb, bearing the effigies of Richard Fitzalan, the Earl of Arundel, who died in 1376, and his countess. The tomb stands in the north aisle of the nave. The Earl's feet rest on a lion; his lady's on a dog.

was rebuilt by the eminent Victorian architect, Sir Gilbert Scott, after it collapsed in 1861 following a severe storm. The beginning of the twentieth century saw the rebuilding of the north-west tower which had crumbled and fallen as long ago as 1635.

A unique feature of Chichester is its fifteenth century free-standing bell tower. It contains a ring of eight bells: two from the sixteenth century, three from the seventeenth and three from the early eighteenth.

The cathedral's most precious possession is a pair of twelfth century stone carvings. Originally coloured, these carvings depicting Christ at the raising of Lazarus and at the gates of Bethany, are situated on the right of the south choir aisle. They were placed there in 1829 after having been found behind the choir stalls, and are probably the finest examples of medieval carving in Britain.

One of Chichester's most interesting features is a John Piper tapestry hung behind the altar from a sixteenth century screen. The tapestry, divided into seven strips, symbolizes the Trinity and was installed in 1966 after being woven in France. Another fine piece of modern art is the Graham Sutherland painting of Mary Magdalen and the risen Christ. It hangs in the Mary Magdalen Chapel where it blends well with the altar rails, candlesticks and book-rest cast in aluminium by Geoffrey Clarke.

Among the many tombs and plaques is a marble memorial to the noted eighteenth century Chichester poet, William Collins, and the fourteenth century Arundel tomb which bears effigies of Richard Fitzalan, Earl of Arundel and his countess.

Right: Some of the finest examples of medieval stone carving to be found in Britain are in Chichester Cathedral. This 12th century stone carving of Christ at the raising of Lazarus is one of two carvings in the south choir aisle.

Coventry

Coventry Cathedral is one of the twentieth century's most imaginative, significant and moving buildings. Its combination of a fourteenth century shell and a dramatic new main structure ensure for this – and future – generations its deserved place as a classic architectural concept.

The old cathedral was destroyed by fire one terrible November night in 1940 when the city of Coventry was laid waste by enemy high explosive and incendiary bombs. All that remained after the holocaust were the blackened outer walls and – as if by a miracle – the magnificent 295 feet high tower and spire.

Within sixteen years Elizabeth II laid the foundation stone of Sir Basil Spence's new cathedral – he won the commission in an open competition – and on May 25th 1962 the building was consecrated. It had cost £1,350,000 and during the eight years it took to build there was not a single industrial dispute among its 500 workers.

The cathedral is now almost as well known for the astounding works of art it contains as it is for its design. Undoubtedly the most striking of these is Graham Sutherland's great tapestry *Christ in Glory* set above and behind the High Altar. The tapestry, the gift of an anonymous Coventry citizen, is the largest in the world, 75 feet by 34 feet, and dominates the entire cathedral.

Another immense feature is the curved Baptistry Window. Designed by John Piper and made by Patrick Reyntiens, its multi-coloured glass and patterned mullions represent an abstract ideal of the light of the Holy Spirit. At the foot of this mighty window, which extends from floor to ceiling, is the font. This is a

Right: This unique Cross, made of silver gilt, rests on the hammered concrete High Altar. Behind it is the incomparable Christ in Glory tapestry by Graham Sutherland.

Opposite: The incredible curved Baptistry Window is yet another of Coventry Cathedral's unique features. At its base is the font, a huge, mis-shapen hunk of sandstone.
Overleaf: A dramatic illustration of the combination of old and new; the burnt-out, 14th century shell wedded to the 20th century creation of Sir Basil Spence.

Right: Sir Jacob Epstein's forceful and effective bronze sculpture of St Michael gaining victory over the Devil. It overlooks the main entrance to the cathedral.

rough, mis-shapen sandstone boulder hewn from the Barakat Valley near Bethlehem.

Opposite, on the other side of the nave, is the circular Chapel of Unity. Designed in the form of a crusader's tent, the chapel has long slender stained glass windows and a beautiful mosaic marble floor.

The main entrance to the cathedral – which is built south to north unlike older ones which run west to east – is through the great canopied porch linking the old and new buildings. It is approached from the east up the broad sweep of St Michael's Steps, overlooked by Sir Jacob Epstein's incomparable bronze sculpture of St Michael subduing the Devil.

From the porch the ruins are reached by the Queen's Steps. The sanctuary contains Coventry's most poignant relic: two charred roof beams tied together in the shape of a cross with the words 'Father Forgive' carved into the stones behind. At the foot of the cross is another. It is made from two of the fourteenth century hand forged nails which literally rained from the roof as the old cathedral perished.

Durham

Despite the fact that Durham was largely built in the remarkably short time of forty years it is deservedly regarded as Britain's finest Norman cathedral.

Impressively situated on a rocky hill high above a loop in the River Wear, Durham stands on a site once occupied by a tenth century church built to house the shrine of Cuthbert, the shepherd boy who became a saint.

In 1093 Bishop William tore down the Anglo-Saxon edifice and laid the foundations of the new cathedral. He died three years later leaving his successor, Bishop Flambard, to continue the work. By this time the choir was finished, the stone vaulting in the aisles being the oldest of its kind in Europe. When Flambard died in 1128 no bishop was appointed to take his place for five years. So, during the interim period, the monks themselves took over. By 1133 they had finished

Below: The cathedral cloisters. These were heavily restored in 1827, losing much of their original charm.

the nave, the aisles and the stone vaulting, this last being one of Durham's most outstanding features.

The nave is richly decorated, the great pillars incised with deep channels in a most unusual way. A short distance inside the nave a black marble slab marks the spot beyond which women were once forbidden. St Cuthbert it seemed disliked women and none were allowed to approach his shrine.

Durham owes its development to the veneration accorded to St Cuthbert. At one time his shrine was reputed to be the most magnificent in Christendom, heaped with jewels, silver and gold. All this, however, disappeared in 1540 when the cathedral surrendered to the crown. What remains lies behind the High Altar, a plain stone slab marking the saint's burial place. His coffin was opened several times down through the centuries and each time it was reported that the body lay uncorrupted.

St Cuthbert is also commemorated in a magnificent twelfth century painting hanging in the Galilee Chapel, where it looks down on the sixteenth century tomb of the Venerable Bede – monk, historian and scholar – who died at Jarrow in 735. The chapel was built in the twelfth century and altered in the fifteenth when its graceful marble shafts were joined by those of stone.

The whole of Durham's interior is lavishly decorated although the screen behind the High Altar – presented by John, Lord Neville in 1380 – has now lost the 107 statues it once contained. The choir stalls are three centuries younger and ornately carved.

The Bishop's Throne, reputedly the highest in any cathedral, surmounts the extravagant tomb erected by its occupant, Bishop Hatfield. He presided at Durham from 1318 to 1333.

On the north-west door is an interesting reminder of medieval days: a sanctuary knocker. Criminals clutching at it could claim sanctuary – and immunity for their offence – for up to 37 days.

Opposite and overleaf: 'half church of God, half castle 'gainst the Scot' – Sir Walter Scott's apt description of Durham Cathedral.
Below: The sanctuary knocker. Any criminal reaching it was given immunity for 37 days.

Above: Part of the priceless Anglo-Saxon stole found in the coffin of St Cuthbert, the north country's most renowned saint.
Left: This reclining figure marks one of Durham's many tombs. The adjacent pillars bear indentations peculiar to the cathedral.

Edinburgh
St Giles' Cathedral

St Giles, the High Kirk of Edinburgh, Scotland's capital city, has a history stretching back more than 1000 years. However, it has been greatly altered and restored down through the centuries, not always happily.

If some of its original overall splendour has been lost, St Giles still retains an impressive interior, its celebrated square central tower with the miniature steeple supported by flying buttresses and – above all – an abiding sense of history.

There was a small church here in the ninth century. When the Normans arrived they built their own church which in turn was destroyed in 1385 when Richard II led a raiding party into Scotland. All that was left were the four immense central pillars.

Two years later the rebuilding started and continued until the latter years of

Left: A floodlit view of St Giles's Crown Steeple supported by its flying buttresses.

Opposite: The Thistle Chapel. Built to serve the Knights of the Thistle, Scotland's oldest order of chivalry, it surprisingly dates from only 1911.

Below: St Giles from the west front. It opens directly onto Edinburgh's High Street, better known as the Royal Mile.

the fifteenth century. In 1454 the kirk was presented with a precious relic, the arm bone of St Giles, a French holy man. However, in 1557, following the Reformation, an ornate gilded statue of St Giles was tossed into the waters of the Nor' Loch below the castle. In 1559 the formidable John Knox became minister of St Giles and within a short time all the old Roman Catholic altars and 'graven images' had been swept away. The walls were whitewashed and the kirk subsequently divided into three separate churches. It remained partitioned until 1872. Knox died in 1572 and is buried in a simple grave at the back of St Giles.

A restoration was carried out between 1829 and 1833 but it did more harm than good. Many of the ancient side chapels and a large part of the west section suffered irreparable damage at the hands of the well-meaning but misguided 'restorers'. It was only the later intervention of William Chambers, publisher and Lord Provost of Edinburgh, that saved St Giles from total desolation. His own work was completed in 1883.

St Giles contains innumerable memorials to famous Scots. They include the

Right: The Marquis of Montrose's monument. It was erected in 1888 to commemorate the Captain-General of Charles I's forces in Scotland. He was executed in 1650 after having been found guilty of treason.

Marquis of Montrose's monument in the Chapman Aisle and an elaborate tomb erected for the first Marquis of Argyll, the covenanter who was executed in 1661 a few years after he himself had been largely responsible for the death of Montrose. The Robert Louis Stevenson memorial in the Moray Aisle Chapel commemorates the great writer.

One of the kirk's most interesting features is the Thistle Chapel, built as recently as 1911 and famous as the most ornate building in Scotland since the Middle Ages. It was designed by Sir Robert Lorrimer for the Knights of the Thistle, Scotland's oldest and grandest order of chivalry, and contains some impressive heraldic glass, wood carving and a particularly elaborate ceiling.

There is also a colourful stained glass window near the Albany Aisle. It was made by the pre-Raphaelite William Morris from a design by Burne-Jones.

Ely

When the central tower of Ely Cathedral collapsed in 1322 after standing for more than 200 years it was replaced with a structure that is unique in European cathedral architecture: a great stone octagon topped with a wooden lantern rising from its centre.

Its creator was a man of vision, imagination and engineering ability far ahead of his time. Faced with the gaping hole, Alan of Walsingham, the sacrist, decided against restoring the original tower, opting instead for the revolutionary octagon. First he built eight massive pillars of stone at each corner. Then, after combing England for trees of the right size, he finally settled for eight oaks weighing ten tons each and trimmed to 63 feet in length. These were to be the corner posts of the lantern.

The lantern tower itself, a construction of timber triangles, rises 60 feet and weighs a total of 400 tons. Such was the genius of Walsingham and his craftsmen that the entire structure rests on the stone pillars with a sheer perpendicular downward thrust. At the base of the octagon arches are the carved stone heads of those involved in its construction.

The Lady Chapel, completed in the mid-fourteenth century, sometime after the octagon, is the largest such chapel in England and its roof span of 46 feet gives it the

Below: The cathedral, looking east to west. The timber lantern rising from the ingenious central octagon is plainly visible.

Above: Rainwater is carried clear of the cathedral walls by grotesquely modelled gargoyles.
Above right: A detail from the stained glass window in the south transept.
Opposite: The view up into the great octagon *amply demonstrates the skill of the medieval craftsmen who built it when the central tower collapsed in 1322.*
Overleaf: Ely from the west front. The entrance is through the beautiful 13th century Galilee Porch.

widest medieval stone vault. Unhappily the Reformation destroyed much of the chapel's original charm: the stained glass windows were smashed and the sculpture and carvings ruined. However, what was spared is still worthy of attention, especially the arcade below the windows.

There is still a good deal of exquisite carving throughout the cathedral, particularly in the south-west transept. The Prior's Door, opening onto the cloisters from the nave, is a fine example of late Norman craftmanship while the fourteenth century choir stalls boast 62 superb misericords.

The west front entrance to Ely is through the lovely Galilee Porch dating from the thirteenth century. From here the entire length of the cathedral is impressively visible, along the narrow Norman nave with its nineteenth century roof paintings to the great stained glass window behind the presbytery and high altar at the east end.

Ely's oldest item is Ovin's Stone, the base of a cross and the only reminder that the cathedral has Saxon origins. The shrine of St Ethelreda contains the relics of Ely's foundress, a remarkable woman who was married to King Egfrid of Northumbria before becoming a nun and later Abbess of Ely.

Of the chantry chapels the most elaborate is Bishop Alcock's, the founder of Jesus College, Cambridge. Bishop West's chantry with its beautiful ceiling is also noteworthy. The finest of the monuments is that erected to the Earl of Worcester beheaded in the Wars of the Roses. It has a triple canopy and stands in the south choir aisle.

During the nineteenth century there was a great deal of restoration, both outside and inside the cathedral. Sir Gilbert Scott was in charge and apart from the insertion of some indifferent Victorian glass, did much to improve Ely's then fading glory.

Exeter

The interior of Exeter Cathedral is, without doubt, one of England's architectural glories. The richness and abundance of its stained glass and window tracery, the detailed woodwork and the decorative stonework is rarely equalled and virtually never excelled. The roof is the longest uninterrupted stretch of Gothic vaulting in the world: 300 feet of soaring stone supported on 30 moulded marble columns and looking not unlike some great avenue of stately trees.

The cathedral's exterior, while not matching the splendour inside, is still impressive. The west front with its niched statues of saints and monarchs is the most interesting although the depredations of age and weather have done much to reduce the overall effect.

Exeter's site dates back as far as 670 when it was used for a small monastery. This was replaced 200 years later by a minster which itself was destroyed by the Danes in 1003. King Canute rebuilt the minster in 1019 and in 1050 Leofric was enthroned as the See of Exeter's first Bishop. He died in 1072, bequeathing a famous set of books to the cathedral library.

Following the Norman Conquest, Exeter grew in importance and it was

Left: Exeter Cathedral, showing the exterior flying buttresses.

decided to extend and alter the existing buildings in keeping with the See's increasing influence. Work started in 1107 on what was to become a unique feature: two great transeptal towers – one on each side of the great structure instead of both in the centre – and in 1133 the new Norman edifice was consecrated. However, apart from the towers, little now remains from the Norman period.

The creation of the cathedral as we know it today was started in 1275 by Bishop Bronescombe. He built the Lady Chapel and the two adjacent chapels. His successor, Bishop Quivil, considerably enhanced the Lady Chapel and opened up the Norman towers, converting them into transepts with huge decorated windows. Thereafter each bishop who followed left his own distinctive impression, culminating with Bishop Grandisson who, among other achievements, completed the Gothic vaulting in the mid-fourteenth century.

Exeter suffered during the Reformation when a great deal of the decoration was either defaced or burnt. The seventeenth century Commonwealth Government added to the damage as did a series of devastating air raids in 1942. Thanks to devoted fund-raising and the dedication of craftsmen, Exeter is now restored – particularly on the inside – to its former magnificence.

As well as being a wonderful work of architecture, Exeter contains so many rare and exquisite treasures that it is impossible to list them all here. They include elaborately carved tombs, painted panels, a fourteenth century minstrel's gallery and a late fifteenth century clock which shows the earth at the centre of the dial with the sun and moon revolving around the outer circle.

Other outstanding features are the carved oak Bishop's Throne, completed in 1312 and standing 60 feet high, the Speke Chantry and the great east window, rebuilt in 1390 from the original of 1303.

Opposite: Looking east down Exeter's nave. It boasts the world's longest unbroken stretch of Gothic vaulting, 300 feet of grace and splendour.
Overleaf: Although Exeter's west front has worn considerably it still presents an impressive facade.

Below: A few of the innumerable niched statues once painted in brilliant colours, which line the west front.

Gloucester

In 1327 when Gloucester – then an abbey – seemed to be heading once more for bankruptcy, the monks accepted the body of the horribly murdered Edward II for burial. It had already been refused at Bristol and Malmesbury.

This hitherto rare display of financial acumen paid off. Once the funeral obsequies were over and Edward laid to rest, his tomb – and more importantly, Gloucester – became such a focus of pilgrimage that it was soon almost impossible to accommodate the crowds.

The abbey began deriving an enormous income from the pilgrims' offerings and it was not long before the money was put to good use – an extensive rebuilding programme. The rebuilding was carried out in the little known Perpendicular style making Gloucester, when it was finished, the birthplace of English Perpendicular Gothic architecture.

Work started in the transepts and choir. The old roof was removed, the east end apse pulled down and a vast perpendicular stone screen was taken up the inside of the Norman arcade, windows were inserted in the screen and a great lierne vault, 92 feet from the ground, erected over the whole. The apse was replaced with an immense stained glass window, 72 feet by 38 feet, the largest of its kind in the country. It dates from the mid-fourteenth century and commemorates those who fought at the Battle of Crécy in 1346.

Below: The fan vaulting in Gloucester's Great Cloister is unique in extent and complexity. Opposite: The cathedral from the east.

Opposite: Edward II's tomb is surmounted by this fine alabaster effigy. The tomb was erected by Edward III in memory of his murdered father.

Right: The reredos, or screen, behind the High Altar. It was designed by Sir Gilbert Scott in the 19th century.

In the centre of the presbytery, and overlooked by the Crecy Window, is the unusual tomb of Robert, Duke of Normandy, William the Conqueror's eldest son. His effigy, in wood, was made towards the end of the thirteenth century while the sarcophagus – also in wood – is fifteenth century. Robert died at Cardiff Castle in 1134 after being held a prisoner for 28 years by his brother, Henry I.

The beautiful canopied tomb of Edward II, with its forest of pinnacles and exquisite alabaster effigy, is to be found under the north arcade of the presbytery. It was erected by his son Edward III and is by far the most notable of the tombs in the cathedral.

It stands not too far from the Lady Chapel which was completed in 1499, marking the final flowering of Gloucester's perpendicular style. Almost the entire wall surface is filled with glass while its vaulted roof is supported on a series of graceful stone arches.

Gloucester's magnificent central tower was built in the mid-fifteenth century to replace one from the thirteenth century. It is 225 feet high and contains the only medieval great bell left in England.

On the north of the cathedral is the Great Cloister. Its fan-vaulting is believed to be unique, the first of such size and complexity built in England.

Hereford

Tradition has it that when King Ethelbert of East Anglia had his head struck off by Offa, King of Mercia in 794, his ghost demanded burial at Hereford. It is believed that a wooden church was erected over the tomb containing his body but this was succeeded in 825 by one of stone.

This in turn was replaced slightly more than two hundred years later and then, in 1056, it was burnt to the ground by Welsh and Irish raiders. In 1080 Robert de Lonsinga began the Norman restoration which was to continue until 1199 when the Early English style started to come to the fore. That in turn gave way to medieval or Decorated Gothic and finally, from the mid-fourteenth century, Perpendicular.

Hereford has had, therefore, a fairly complicated architectural history. This was aggravated by a questionable building programme undertaken by James Wyatt following the collapse of the west tower in 1786. This gave him the opportunity to destroy much of the original Norman work – especially in the nave – and resulted in a new and somewhat incongruous west front which between 1902 and 1908 was replaced with the present neo-Gothic facade.

None of this, however, detracts in any way from the impact of the splendidly dignified central tower. This, together with the now sadly lost Chapter House,

Opposite: Hereford Cathedral, looking towards the west front, sadly much damaged by Wyatt's programme of restoration during the 18th century.

Below: The cathedral library contains many treasures, including this exquisitely decorated Limoges enamel Becket reliquary dating from the 13th century.

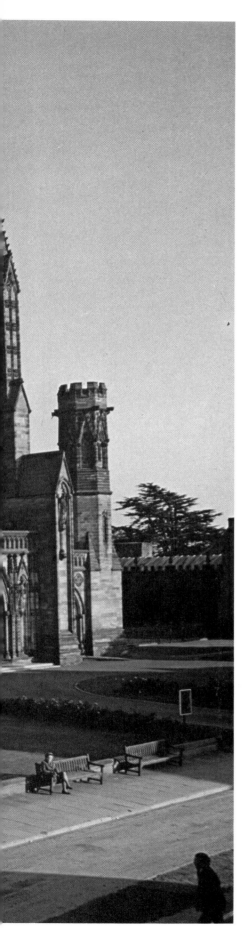

Above: This crucifix which decorates the tomb of Peter Aquablanca (Bishop of Hereford from 1240 to 1268) is the only one to have survived the depredations of Cromwell's troops during the English Civil War.

Right: The chantry of John Stanbury, Bishop of Hereford from 1453 to 1474, is an exquisite example of decorative medieval architecture.

dates from the early fourteenth century and stands on the old Norman piers and arches. Until 1790 it had a lead-covered timber spire.

One of the cathedral's most beautiful interior features is the early thirteenth century Lady Chapel. Its five narrow lancet windows at the east end, set in elaborate frames, lend the chapel a special dignity. The reredos behind the altar was presented to Hereford in 1951: its panels, depicting the life of Mary, together with the separate figures of Ethelbert and St Cantelupe, Bishop of Hereford from 1275 to 1282, make it a worthy modern addition to an ancient setting.

Among Hereford's many treasures, probably the most unusual is the *Mappa Mundi*, which hangs in the north aisle of the choir. A unique late thirteenth century map of the world, it is drawn on vellum and shows Jerusalem at the centre. Close by is the Stanbury Tomb and Chantry. Stanbury, a Bishop of Hereford in the mid-fifteenth century was Henry VI's Confessor as well as being a distinguished architect having drawn up the plans for the chapel at Eton. His tomb and effigy is in alabaster while the chantry, opposite, is richly decorated.

There are nearly 1500 books in the cathedral's famous chained library situated off the cloisters. The books are chained to seventeenth century oak bookcases and it is the largest – and probably the finest – such library in the world. The oldest and most valuable book is the Anglo-Saxon Gospels, written in Latin during the last years of the eighth century. Also on display in the library is the thirteenth Beckett Reliquary in Limogés enamel.

Lichfield

Although Lichfield is one of England's smaller cathedrals its three magnificent and unique spires – the Ladies of the Vale – certainly make it one of the most distinctive. The central and tallest spire, rising to a height of 258 feet, was rebuilt in the second half of the seventeenth century after it had been destroyed by Cromwell's pitiless cannon. But the matching pair over the elaborate west front have survived since 1320.

The earliest cathedral at Lichfield was built in 700 to house the wooden shrine of St Chad, Bishop of Mercia from 669 to 672. Nothing, however, remains from those far off days neither does much from the first Norman building of 1140.

Lichfield as we know it today was built largely between 1195 and 1325 as a direct response to the crowds of pilgrims making their way to St Chad's Shrine. The old building proved too small to accommodate them and was pulled down. The earliest part of the new cathedral was the choir, built in the Early English style

Below: One of Lichfield Cathedral's most treasured possessions – St Chad's Gospel, an illuminated manuscript book written in the eighth century.

and restored in the nineteenth century by Sir Gilbert Scott. He installed the stalls and the equally ornate Bishop's Throne.

The nave was completed in 1258 and, apart from the roof, is unchanged. It is a particularly fine example of Early English architecture combined with that of the Decorated period.

At the far end of the nave is the exquisite Lady Chapel, built in the early fourteenth century. Its chief interest lies in seven of the nine stained glass windows at the apsidal east end. They are sixteenth century Flemish and were bought from Herckenrode Abbey, Belgium, in 1802.

As has already been stated, Cromwell's cannon gave Lichfield a terrible battering in the seventeenth century. The only part of the roof to survive was that over the thirteenth century Chapter House with its 13 canopied stalls. The upper part – the capital – of the central column was carved by four different craftsmen each of whom, as can be seen, indulged his own preference. The column carries on up into the second storey of the Chapter House known as the Treasury, but in fact used as the cathedral library.

The library contains Lichfield's greatest treasure: St Chad's Gospel, written and illuminated in the first years of the eighth century. It includes the complete Gospels of St Mark and St Matthew and is one of the finest manuscripts of its kind in Europe.

Lichfield's west front was extensively restored in the nineteenth century and unfortunately only five of the original thirteenth century statues are now left. These are situated in the north-west tower. All the rest are Victorian reproductions.

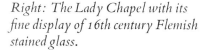

Right: The Lady Chapel with its fine display of 16th century Flemish stained glass.

Opposite: Lichfield Cathedral's richly decorated west front. It was restored extensively in the 19th century.

Lincoln

On April 15 1185 an unusual and totally unexpected earthquake shattered Lincoln's Norman cathedral buildings. All that was left standing were the two west towers and the west front. However, only seven years later rebuilding began and resulted in what is arguably Britain's finest cathedral.

The work started with the choir and the east transepts, continued with the main transepts, the chapter house, central tower and nave and finished with the cloisters, presbytery and retro-choir in the late thirteenth century.

This last – the retro-choir – is known as the Angel Choir and is Lincoln's main glory. It was built, surprisingly enough, by demolishing some of the first work at the east end of the cathedral. Whatever whim or architectural vagary dictated the decision, it left Lincoln – and the rest of the country – with the ultimate expression of English Gothic.

The Angel Choir houses an elaborate plinth on which a silver casket containing the head of St Hugh, the bishop who rebuilt Lincoln after the earthquake, used to stand. His coffin and shrine, once the object of pilgrims' veneration, has long since disappeared. There is some magnificent carving and sculpture, particularly the 30 angels between the shoulders of the ornate arches which line the triforium, or upper part of the wall, opening onto a gallery. The last shoulder on the north side contains a mischievous little figure known popularly as the 'Lincoln Imp'. He is shown emerging from a carving of foliage.

Another of Lincoln's fine features is its stained glass. The earliest is the great rose window, or Dean's Eye, at the north end of the great transept. It dates back to the early thirteenth century and has been longer in its setting than any other glass in the country. Opposite, at the other end of the transept is the Bishop's Eye. This bewilderingly complex display of medieval glass separated by flowing decorated tracery, was restored at the end of the eighteenth century.

It would take a week to see all the treasures of Lincoln, just as it would take a complete book to describe them. Everywhere you look there is a profusion of

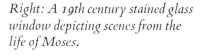

Right: A 19th century stained glass window depicting scenes from the life of Moses.

Opposite: Lincoln's chief glory, the 13th-century Angel Choir.

wonderfully worked glass, stone and wood. The fourteenth century choir stalls and their superb misericords deserve special attention, as does the extraordinarily intricate pulpitum or choir screen.

Historically speaking the Chapter House is of especial interest. It was here in February 1301, while presiding over a Parliamentary session, that Edward I created his eldest son the Prince of Wales.

From the outside the west front is a splendid combination of the original Norman structure and Bishop Hugh's new building. There are the statues of 11 English kings above the central doorway while the turrets on either side of the front each has its own single statue: one is of Bishop Hugh and the other is the Swineherd of Stowe, a man who gave the cathedral every penny he possessed.

The two towers over the west front are 206 feet high while the central tower reaches 271 feet. It houses a five-and-a-half ton bell called 'Great Tom of Lincoln'. The central tower, rebuilt in the fourteenth century after the collapse of an earlier one, was once topped by a wooden spire. This gave it a total height of 524 feet, the highest in the country. However, it was wrecked by a storm in 1584 and never replaced.

Right: The west front.
Opposite: Lincoln Cathedral's central tower. Once topped by a wooden spire, it was never replaced after its collapse in 1584.
Overleaf: A few of the grotesque carved figures on the cathedral exterior.

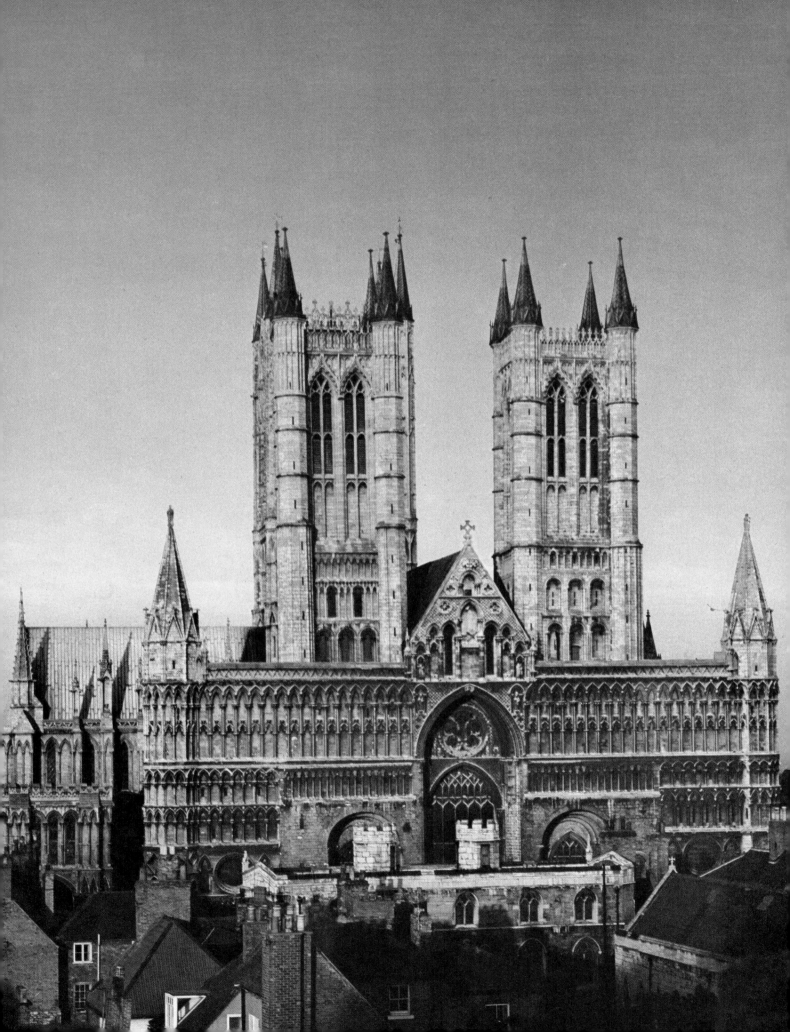

Liverpool

Everything about Liverpool Cathedral is on the grand scale. From its mighty central tower to the incredible 9000 pipe organ, it is massive. This is the twentieth century's answer to the medieval builders: it was started in 1904 and when finished shortly, will be the world's largest cathedral after St Peter's in Rome.

The architect, Sir Giles Gilbert Scott – grandson of the renowned restorer of Gothic churches – was only 22 when he won the commission in competition with more than 100 aspirants. On July 19th 1904 Edward VII laid the foundation stone. Six years later the first part of the new cathedral, the Lady Chapel, was consecrated.

It is a very ornately decorated structure and differs from other Lady Chapels in that it projects from the south-east corner of the building, rather than extending directly behind the high altar. The stained glass windows commemorate various women, Biblical, historical and contemporary, while the screen behind the altar depicts the Nativity.

The First World War impeded progress but did not halt it entirely and the next part of the cathedral, the choir, eastern transepts and Chapter House, was consecrated in 1924.

Almost immediately afterwards the War Memorial Chapel and the Cenotaph were dedicated. The Cenotaph is made of richly carved wood and black fossil marble. It bears the Roll of Honour, an illuminated book now containing nearly forty thousand names. This is already regarded as one of Liverpool's most treasured possessions.

The work continued apace until being slowed by the Second World War

Left: Liverpool Cathedral's highly decorated and gilded High Altar. Its central feature is a study of the Last Supper.

when the craftsmen and labourers dwindled away to a mere handful. In 1941 the central space under the tower and the west transepts were finished. Then, eight years later the central Vestey tower and the north and south porches reached completion. The tower is easily the cathedral's most dominant feature. It is 347 feet high and houses the heaviest peal of bells in the world. There are 14 altogether, 13 of which are grouped round the immense Bourdon – the bell with the lowest key – which weighs an incredible 14½ tons.

Another of the cathedral's unique features is the east window of the choir. It is the largest in the country, 76 feet by 44 feet, and takes the Te Deum as its theme. Under the window is the lavishly carved and gilded high altar, the reredos of which is actually a part of the wall itself – most unusual in cathedral architecture.

This is the first Gothic cathedral to have been built since the Reformation. It is an achievement that many thought impossible – the resurrection of the medieval ideal using modern skills and imagination.

Llandaff

The nave of Llandaff is dominated by a great concrete arch supporting an equally impressive cylindrical organ case. The sides of the case are decorated with 64 gilded pre-Raphaelite figures while the front provides the setting for Epstein's vast figure of Christ cast in unpolished aluminium. The whole concept is incredibly effective, not least because it is so unexpected in what is essentially a medieval church.

Despite this uncompromising concession to modernity, Llandaff has a history which stretches back further than any English cathedral. It was founded around 560 by Teilo, a missionary who took the name from a nearby river. Nothing now remains of the sixth century Christian outpost, nor does anything of a later church which stood on the site until the beginning of the twelfth century.

In 1120 a Norman bishop called Urban began building a new church, starting with the presbytery and choir. The dignified arch leading from behind the High

Left: The nave, dominated by the great aluminium statue of Christ by Epstein.

Right: Llandaff Cathedral from the south-east. Following the devastation caused by a German landmine in 1941 the building was more or less totally restored.

Altar to the Lady Chapel is a noteworthy survivor from this period. It is overlooked by a window designed by John Piper.

The Lady Chapel itself was built during the thirteenth century and has a particularly fine vaulted ceiling. It contains the tomb of William de Braose, bishop from 1266 to 1287.

Llandaff was sadly neglected after the Reformation and by the time Cromwell's soldiers used the nave as a beer house in the mid-seventeenth century, the cathedral was in a very sorry state. However, worse was to come. Storms in 1703 and 1723 brought down pinnacles, the south-west tower and the nave roof. Soon the once-proud building lay in virtual ruins.

A brave attempt at restoration was made in the second half of the eighteenth century but in doing so, much of the medieval structure was lost. Then, in 1835 a major restoration began and continued until 1869. During those 34 years the decaying cathedral regained much of its former dignity. The architect, a local man called John Pritchard, was responsible for some interesting innovations including, along the north and south walls of the nave, the sculpted heads of all the British monarchs from Richard III to Edward VIII. George VI and Elizabeth II were later added to the north side.

In January 1941 a German landmine undid the good work, its explosion causing more damage than had been achieved through storms, neglect and the Civil War. Llandaff was more or less sealed off – after Coventry the worst hit cathedral of the war.

But by August 1960, Llandaff was totally – and imaginatively – restored and its old features once more displayed. These include a Rosseti painting *The Seed of David* which forms a triptych in the Illtyd Chapel; the thirteenth century shrine of St Teilo and a series of Pre-Raphaelite porcelain panels in the Chapel of St Dyfig depicting the six days of the Creation.

Londonderry
St Columb's Church of Ireland Cathedral

During the famous siege of 1689 when Londonderry defended itself against the forces of King James II, a shell was fired into the cathedral yard. It was soon discovered that the shell contained the expected capitulation terms. A great cry of 'No surrender' split the air. Today, nearly three hundred years later, the words still mean the same but in a different context.

In 1913 the descendants of those who held the city erected a siege window in the vestibule. It depicts the relief of Londonderry after a siege lasting an incredible 105 days which had cost the lives of ten thousand of its citizens. The Chapter House, just off the vestibule, has an exhibition of various objects connected with the city's history, including the padlocks and keys of the gates which the celebrated apprentice boys locked in the face of the enemy.

St Columb's was built by the Irish Society in 1633 using what is now known as the 'Planters' Gothic' style of architecture. The spire was added at the beginning of the nineteenth century and then, towards the end of the century the cathedral was restored and extended. The roof rests on corbels, or stone projections, some of them representing earlier bishops of Londonderry.

Within the cathedral itself there are monuments to some of the seventeenth century 'Planters' – Scots and English immigrants sent over by James I to people Ireland's northern counties. The monument to Alexander Tomkins, an alderman, and his step-father John Elvin who became mayor, is particularly noteworthy.

There is some interesting glass – besides the seige window – including the St Columba window which depicts the saint on his sixth century mission to Britain and another dedicated to the memory of Mrs Frances Alexander, widow of a late nineteenth century bishop. Mrs Alexander is well remembered for her hymns, three of which are illustrated in the glass.

Overleaf: The interior of Londonderry's 17th century St Columb's Cathedral.

Left: An example of 'Planter's Gothic architecture, St Columb's Cathedral was built in 1663.

Manchester

A series of restorations, the last following an air raid in 1940, means that Manchester is now noted rather more for what it contains than for any architectural merit it might once have possessed. And, while it is true that the width of the nave is the greatest in the country – exceeding even York by ten feet – the cathedral's actual area is comparatively small.

Manchester was founded early in the fifteenth century when Henry V granted Thomas de la Warre permission to build a church alongside his existing priests' college. The original charter still hangs in the cathedral. Building began around 1422 and continued until 1522. When it was finished Manchester boasted – as it still does – some of the most magnificent wood carving to be found in any English cathedral.

The most obvious example is the screen dividing the nave from the choir. This screen – or pulpitum – is made of intricately worked solid oak, and has a fine display of painted panels. A new cornice was added in 1872 but it was designed to blend happily with its medieval setting.

Within the choir itself the stalls show early sixteenth century craftsmanship at its incomparable best. Each one of the 30 stalls is surmounted by an ornate canopy supported by elegant shafts. The misericords under the seats are also so cleverly detailed that it seems a pity they remain concealed.

When the fatal bomb fell in 1940 one of the worst hit casualties was the Lady Chapel. Amazingly, however, the screen separating it from the retro-choir was unscathed. This screen was made around 1440 and is the oldest in the cathedral. On the outside wall of the now restored Chapel is a gilded bronze statue of the Virgin and Child by the late Sir Charles Wheeler, one-time President of the Royal Academy. He has depicted her wearing the scarf, shawl and dress of a Lancashire mill girl.

Among the other interesting artistic pieces is a series of murals showing the Beatitudes in modern dress. They were painted by Carel Weight and fill the stone tracery over the double-arched entrance to the Chapter House.

Left: A contemporary picture of the extensive damage to Manchester Cathedral caused by an air raid in 1940.

Opposite: The nave with its elegant camber beam roof, tiled floor and unusually wide clerestroy windows.
Right: The main entrance to Manchester Cathedral.

Bottom right: An enchanting study of a farmer's wife chasing a fox which has made off with a goose forms part of a misericord in the choir stalls.
Below: An Anglo-Saxon stone carving of an angel. It was discovered when the north porch foundations were being dug in the late 19th century.

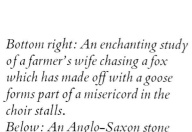

Norwich

The spire of Norwich Cathedral soars 315 feet – second only to Salisbury – while the tower from which it rises is not only the tallest Norman tower in the country but also one of the finest surviving from the Norman period. This, together with the splendidly elegant flying buttresses supporting the presbytery vault, are Norwich's most distinctive exterior features.

The architectural glory of the interior is undoubtedly the perfectly proportioned Norman apse at the cathedral's east end. The apse, or semi-circular cathedral end, is surmounted with a magnificent clerestory rebuilt in the fourteenth century after the original was destroyed when an earlier wooden spire collapsed.

Norwich Cathedral's foundation stone was laid in 1096 by Bishop Herbert de Losinga. By the time he died in 1119 he had completed the presbytery, the transepts, part of the central tower and the east end of the nave. In 1272 the citizens of Norwich rioted and set fire to the cathedral interior and burnt down most of the domestic buildings. The damage was so severe that six years later Norwich was re-consecrated.

Building continued throughout the thirteenth, fourteenth and early years of the fifteenth centuries. Norwich suffered considerably during the Civil War but quickly recovered after the Restoration.

Among the cathedral's various unique features is the fact that the cathedra, or

Right: A detail from a 14th century panel depicting the Ascension in the Ambulatory Chapel.

Opposite: Norwich Cathedral from the south side. The 14th century flying buttresses support the choir clerestory.

Right: The nave is 250 feet long and possesses a magnificent lierne vault built over the Norman walls in the 15th century.

Below: The south nave aisle. It dates mostly from the Norman period.

bishop's throne, is positioned east of the altar. This throne is Norwich's most treasured possession and dates back to the eighth century when the See of East Anglia was established at Dunwich. It is the oldest bishop's throne still used in England and incorporates pieces of stone from the ancient Saxon cathedral.

Norwich also contains what could well be England's oldest religious effigy: it is not certain whom it represents – possibly Losinga – but it is known to date back to around 1100 when it was placed in a niche above the north transept door. In 1968 it was moved into the ambulatory and placed near a seven sacrament fifteenth century font. The ambulatory's south walk leads to the fourteenth century Bauchon Chapel with its particularly fine and ornate bosses.

Other chapels contain exquisite wall panels painted by Norwich artists of the medieval era. The retable – frame of decorated panels at back of altar – in St Luke's is of special note. Just east of St Luke's Chapel is the last resting place of Edith Cavell, the British nurse executed by the Germans in 1915.

Away from the main body of the cathedral are the cloisters, the only two-storeyed monastic cloisters in England. They are also among the finest, with their window tracery and elaborately sculptured vault bosses.

Oxford

Oxford is unique for two reasons: it is the smallest cathedral in England and it is the only cathedral in the world which also serves as a college chapel – namely Christ Church.

It was originally founded as an eighth century nunnery and later rebuilt by the Normans. During the sixteenth century four of the eight nave bays were lost when Cardinal Wolsey wanted more space for the quadrangle of what was to be his Cardinal College. He also partly demolished the cloisters and used the stone – as well as that from the nave – to augment the materials he needed for the college. It is quite probable that had he not fallen from favour with Henry VIII, he would have eventually demolished the entire cathedral.

In 1546 Henry designated the by now much depleted building as cathedral of the new diocese of Oxford and instructed that it should also be used as the chapel of the newly founded Christ Church College.

The exterior, although interesting, is somewhat difficult to see. It is notable chiefly for the thirteenth century spire which is believed to be one of the oldest in the country.

The interior, however, is a delight, despite the fact that it dates from so many different periods. The intriguing double arches in the nave are undoubtedly Norman while the choir, with its exquisite fan vaulting is late fifteenth century. The roof of the nave is sixteenth century timber while that of the lantern is a hundred years earlier.

Left: Burne-Jones, the 19th century artist, designed several of Oxford's Christ Church Cathedral's stained glass windows. This shows a detail from the St Catherine Window.

Overleaf: Although the smallest of England's cathedrals, Christ Church qualifies as one of the most picturesque.

There is some fine fourteenth and seventeenth century glass, the room itself being a magnificent example of thirteenth century architecture.

In the north aisle of the choir is the late thirteenth century leaf-sculpted base of what was once the shrine of St Frideswide, daughter of an eighth century king. An extremely rare fifteenth century wooden watching chamber is close by. St Frideswide's finely restored tomb now lies in the Lady Chapel.

Right: The 15th century fan-vaulted choir.

Opposite: Christ Church Cathedral, Oxford, from the north.

Peterborough

Peterborough shares with Wells the distinction of an incomparable west front. It lacks the extravagant medieval sculpture of its Somerset counterpart but more than compensates by the sheer splendour of its architecture, the dominant feature being three 81 feet high ornate and deeply recessed arches.

The west front, a classic example of the early English design, is 156 feet wide and was built at the beginning of the thirteenth century, masking the earlier Norman facade. The central porch – a somewhat incongruous structure – was added in 1370.

Peterborough did not become a cathedral until the dissolution of the monasteries in the sixteenth century. Previously it was an abbey, with origins dating back to the seventh century. Following Viking raids in 870 when the abbey was burnt and its monks cruelly slaughtered, Peterborough lay in ruins for 100 years. It was eventually rebuilt by Aethelwold, Bishop of Winchester, who claimed he had been asked to do so in a dream. During the next century Peterborough was attacked again – this time by Hereward the Wake as a protest against the appointment of the first Norman bishop. Hereward's raid did not cause too much damage but an accidental fire in 1116 destroyed most of the abbey and its domestic buildings.

Two years later the Normans began to rebuild Peterborough. The work was to continue for 80 years finally resulting in much of what stands today. The nave with its wooden vault is particularly striking. The ceiling was painted around 1220 and is one of the most important pieces of medieval art in existence. It is decorated with saints, kings, monsters and bishops and is one of only four such ceilings left in Europe.

Just inside the west entrance, to the north of the door, is a late sixteenth

Below: Peterborough Cathedral's much restored 13th century west front. The porch was added in the following century.

Right: The interior of the central tower. Built originally by by the Normans it was replaced in the 14th and 19th centuries.

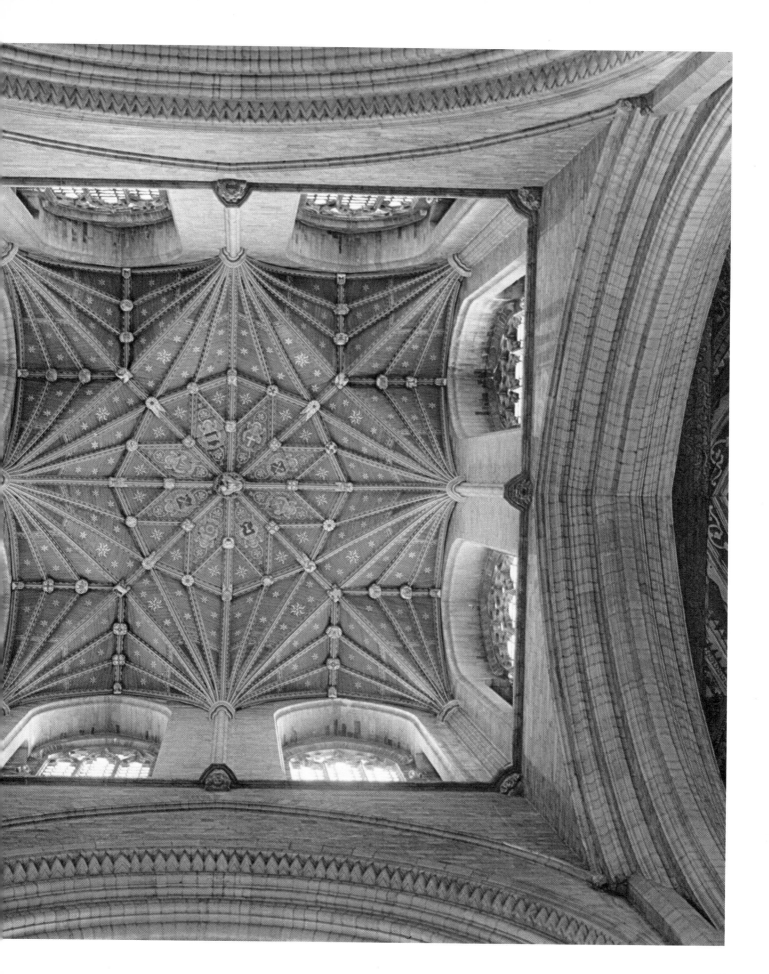

century portrait of Robert Scarlett the sexton who buried Catherine of Aragon and Mary, Queen of Scots. Catherine remains in the cathedral, commemorated by a tomb in the north aisle of the presbytery. Mary's tomb, however, was removed by her son James I in 1612 to a more magnificent setting in Westminster Abbey. The site of her original tomb at Peterborough is marked with a simple stone tablet fixed to a column on the south side of the presbytery.

By the fourteenth century the central tower – like so many Norman towers – had become unsafe. It was taken down and replaced with a lower one, itself rebuilt in 1884. Many of the old materials were used and the result, especially from inside, is pleasing. The wooden vaulted ceiling is painted and decorated. The ceiling of the choir is also richly decorated although many of its fittings – including the stalls and bishop's throne – date from the late nineteenth century.

Following the destruction of the Civil War Peterborough remained in a fairly indifferent state until the early years of the nineteenth century when an extensive programme of restoration was started. A great deal of new Gothic stonework went into the cathedral and the presbytery's fifteenth century painted wooden vault now looks down on stalls and box pews from a much later period.

Right: The south transept. A subway running underneath gives access to the foundations of the 10th century Saxon church.

Ripon

The crypt at Ripon has survived since the seventh century, one of the few Anglo-Saxon ecclesiastical buildings still extant. It is a small cramped place, reached by a stair from the nave. On the north side of the crypt is a narrow hole known as Wilfred's Needle, once used as a test of chastity. Only those slim enough to squeeze through into the passage outside were adjudged pure.

Ninth century Danish raiders reduced the church above the crypt to a ruin but it was rebuilt the following century and declared a place of sanctuary. But any criminal who claimed the right of shelter at Ripon soon found himself before a church court and subsequent trial by ordeal.

The Norman Conquest saw Ripon once more in ruins and it remained so until 1080 when Thomas of Bayeux, Archbishop of York began to rebuild. The vaulted undercroft beneath the Chapter House – now a mortuary chapel – remains from this period as does the apsidal east end of the Chapter House itself.

Ripon as we know it today dates from 1154 and the arrival at York of Archbishop Roger Pont l'Eveque. During the 27 years before his death he built Ripon into what is now a classic example of the Transitional Norman style.

His successors continued the work, notably Walter de Grey, who contributed the somewhat severe west front with its twin towers. These were originally topped with wooden spires sheathed in lead but they were removed in 1664 as four years earlier the spire of the central tower had collapsed for the second time.

The much restored rather squat central tower now provides – internally – one of Ripon's outstanding architectural features: it has two round and two pointed arches, a direct result of the fifteenth century builders' failure to finish remodelling the tower. They managed to complete the two on the south and east sides in the pointed Perpendicular style but left those on the north and west as round twelfth century Norman Transitional.

Other features include the beautiful canopied fifteenth century choir stalls, the stone bosses in the choir ceiling and the remarkable twentieth century reredos, a memorial to the men of Ripon who died in the First World War.

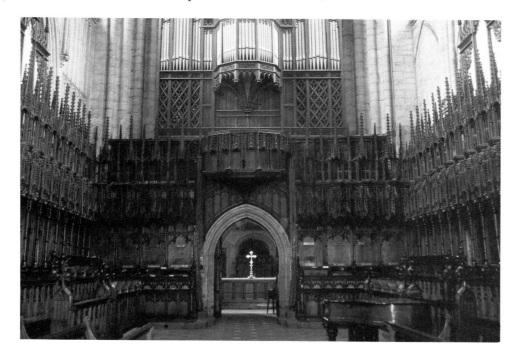

Left: The 15th century canopied choir stalls, among Ripon Cathedral's most interesting and attractive features. The central organ case was designed by Sir Gilbert Scott in 1860.

Overleaf: The squat towers of Ripon tend to make the cathedral look rather lower than its actual height.

Rochester

The ancient Saxon cathedral at Rochester had served the community for over four hundred years before a new Norman bishop was installed in 1077. Bishop Gundulph, seeing the neglected condition of the cathedral, decided to rebuild it to his own plans.

Gundulph's first priority was a 50 feet high, massively strong, stone tower. As the architect of London's White Tower and Rochester Castle, Gundulph was well-versed in military matters and it is presumed he intended that the tower should be used for defensive purposes – should the need arise. It still stands situated rather incongruously between the two transepts on the north side of the cathedral.

Building on the cathedral proper began in 1080, starting with a raised choir and presbytery at the eastern end. Gundulph died before his work was done but his splendid nine-bay nave – although incomplete – must have seemed a worthy monument. Two later bishops finished the nave and considerably extended the

Below: A complete view of Rochester Cathedral, looking down on it from the west.

west front. Much of Gundulph's earlier work was re-cased with better stone, imported from Caen.

The west front door was built in the mid-twelfth century and is considered one of the finest in England. With its elaborate sculptured tympanum – semi-circular stonework over a door or window – and its receding arches, the door is probably Rochester's most outstanding feature. The much-weathered statues of Henry I and Queen Matilda positioned on either side of the door are reputed to be the earliest such statues still in existence.

In 1179 most of the city of Rochester was levelled by fire – the second since 1137 – and the cathedral was badly damaged. Fortunately the nave arcades and the walls of the choir survived. The east wall in the cloister garth still bears a faint red tinge.

Building and rebuilding continued well into the fifteenth century when the great perpendicular window was inserted in the west front. It was renewed in the nineteenth century and now serves as a memorial to the Royal Engineers who perished in the Afghan and South African wars.

There was some unsympathetic restoration carried out in the nineteenth century but, by and large, Rochester remains a reasonable example of one of the Norman's smaller cathedrals. It contains the usual tombs to successive bishops as well as several interesting wall paintings, including the thirteenth century Wheel of Fortune standing opposite the Bishop's throne in the choir. Among the older parts of the cathedral, the best surviving piece of craftsmanship from the fourteenth century is the beautifully carved and decorated doorway from the south choir transept to the Chapter Room.

Right: The west door demonstrates the skill of Norman craftsmen at their best. It is thought to be one of the finest of its kind in England.

St Albans

St Albans was founded as a Benedictine abbey in 793 to commemorate a Roman soldier who, when he was beheaded nearly 500 years earlier for harbouring a priest, became Britain's first Christian martyr.

The abbey was built on the site where he died, the crown of a hill overlooking the ancient town of Verulamium – now better known as St Albans. By 1088 the first Norman abbot, Paul of Caen, had rebuilt the Saxon abbey using bricks from the ruined Roman town. It was re-dedicated in 1115 and then rebuilt and extended again from 1200 until the year before Magna Carta, when St Albans had become the country's richest monastic house.

Henry VIII proposed that St Albans should become a cathedral when he dissolved the monastries. The townspeople, however, preferred to retain it as a parish church. As such it was far too large and fell into disrepair until 1856 when Sir Gilbert Scott was commissioned to begin a restoration. Then, in 1877, it was created the cathedral of the new diocese of St Albans.

From the exterior there is little to commend St Albans except perhaps the Norman tower. Inside, however, the nave – the longest medieval nave in existence, $257\frac{1}{2}$ feet – does have a certain majesty.

Right: St Albans from the west front. Along with much of the rest of the cathedral the west front was completely rebuilt in the late 19th century by Lord Grimthorpe, a wealthy and somewhat forceful benefactor. He insisted that the restoration be carried out to his own specifications, with not always pleasing results.

Opposite: The decorated wooden vault over the choir was erected in the 13th century and painted with its eagle and lamb motif two centuries later. The reredos beneath dates from 1484; it was restored around 1900.

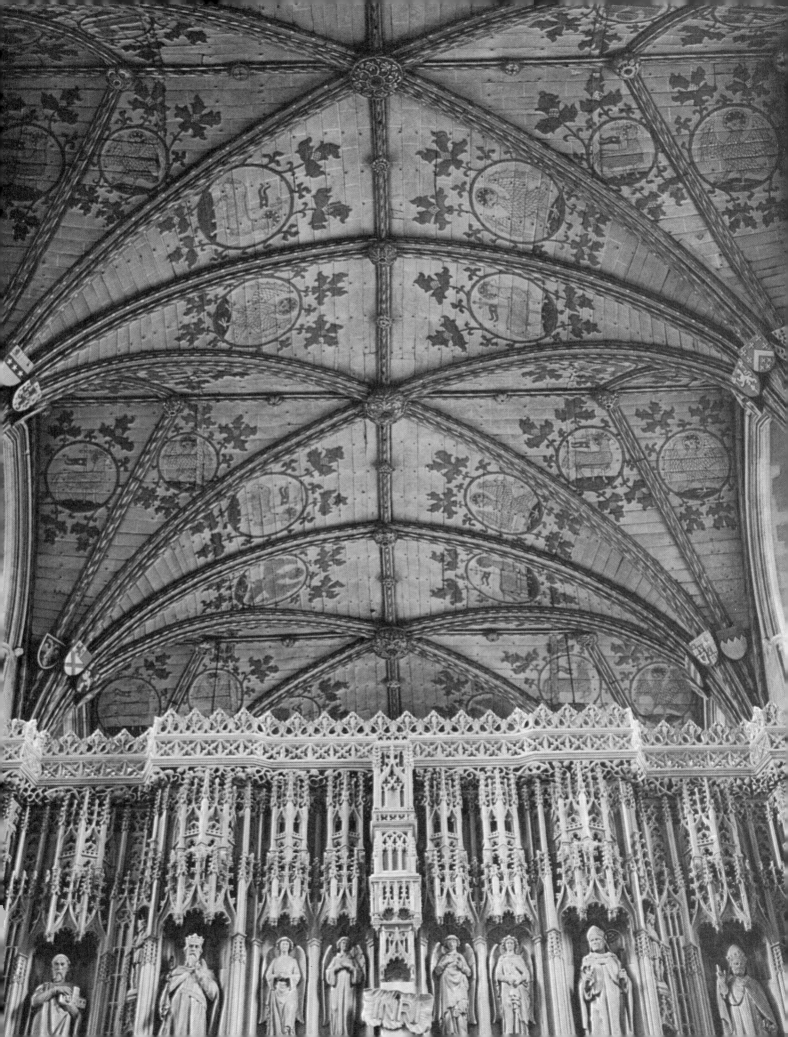

Above: St Albans possesses some fine 13th and 14th century wall paintings. Until fairly recently they were hidden by whitewash. This particular study, of Christ on the Cross, was cleaned in 1955.
Above right: The shrine of St Alban. Behind is the early 15th century watching chamber from which monks kept a wary eye on pilgrims at the shrine.

It contains the remains of thirteenth and fourteenth century wall paintings on west and south sides of the Norman piers. There are also some fine painted panels on the choir ceiling; they have lasted unscathed since the fifteenth century despite once being plastered over. The choir is separated from the nave by a fourteenth century stone rood screen – the only screen of its type in an English cathedral.

The presbytery has a unique wooden vault which was painted in 1450 and is dominated by the vast and incredibly ornate reredos behind the altar. It was erected in the late fifteenth century and extensively restored in the early 1900s. To the east of the presbytery, and behind the high altar, is St Alban's Chapel. This houses the saint's shrine, the base of which was re-assembled in 1872 from about two thousand fragments of the original pedestal found among the rubble of a wall which blocked the arches at the east end of the chapel. On the north side of the chapel is the wooden watching chamber where monks guarded the shrine from over-eager pilgrims. The back of the chamber has delightful carvings of scenes from rural life.

On the south side stands the magnificent thirteenth century tomb of Humphrey, Duke of Gloucester and Henry V's brother. Richly decorated with statuettes, it is covered by a lofty canopy and protected by a wrought-iron Sussex grille.

The Lady Chapel at the east end of the cathedral was completed in the fourteenth century. It was freely restored in the nineteenth century although it still displays its elaborate window tracery and niched effigies.

St Asaph's

St Asaph is the smallest ancient cathedral in England and Wales. However, this has not prevented it from suffering the same misfortunes as the majority of larger British cathedrals.

It was founded as far back as 560 by the missionary St Kentigern after he had been exiled from Scotland. He was succeeded by St Asaph as bishop. The original building was rebuilt by the Normans and then destroyed by the English in the thirteenth century. In the next century it was a Welshman, the warrior Prince Owain Glyndwr who laid it waste.

In 1482 St Asaph was rebuilt yet again and managed to survive until the Civil War when, once more, it suffered considerable damage. In 1714 a fierce storm put paid to the roof and 65 years later the Chapter House was pulled down. The cathedral then lay in ruins until the nineteenth century when it was painstakingly and extensively restored by Sir Gilbert Scott.

The library, or museum, contains several interesting and rare books including the first Welsh translation of the Bible accomplished by Bishop William Morgan in 1588. There is also a display of some fine pieces of sixteenth and seventeenth century silver.

Overleaf: A general view of St Asaph, the smallest cathedral in England and Wales.

Below: The somewhat austere but dignified interior of St Asaph.

St David's

St David's, unlike most other cathedrals, does not dominate its surroundings. Instead it nestles in a hollow, its tranquil sandstone peacefully harmonizing with the backcloth of fields and coastal hills.

This is the oldest cathedral settlement in Britain. It has a continuous history dating back to the mid-sixth century when it served as a remote Welsh outpost of the Christian faith. The founder was Dewi Sant – St David, the patron saint of Wales. He forged such a feeling of religious community and extended the influence of his church so far, that it lasted as a pilgrim centre centuries after his death.

William the Conqueror visited St David's in 1081 but it was not until 1115 that the monks were forced to accept a royal nominee as their bishop. He was called Bernard and, once he had re-organized the monastery's working structure, he started re-building and re-modelling on a modest scale. In 1131 St David's was consecrated. Forty years later Henry II made a pilgrimage there as part of his atonement for Becket's murder by which time St David's income was large enough for the start of three centuries of building.

From the outside the cathedral is conventional enough – if not to say austere –

Left: The restored front of St Davids, with the adjacent medieval chapel.

Opposite: The nave of St Davids contains a mixture of styles and age ranging from the carved oak 16th century roof to the 20th century organ.
Overleaf: The Bishop's Throne. It is graced with three intricate canopies and dates from the early 16th century.

Below: St Davids has never intruded on its surroundings. Instead it nestles modestly in a hollow, blending peacefully with the Welsh landscape.

but this belies the magnificence of the interior. The most immediate and probably the most striking feature is the unique sixteenth century carved Irish oak ceiling. It is profusely and elaborately ornamented, the richness of the decoration contrasting beautifully with the plain unpainted wood surface.

The roof of the presbytery is also splendidly decorated, but in warm glowing colours handpainted in the fourteenth century. It looks down on the somewhat awkwardly placed white stone tomb of Edmund Tudor, the Earl of Richmond. Standing in the centre of the tiled presbytery floor, the tomb is separated from the High Altar by a low rail. Tudor's remains were transferred from the dissolved church of Grey Friars at Carmarthen, on the instructions of his grandson, Henry VIII.

Another interesting feature linking St David's with the monarchy is the medieval royal stall, the only such stall in a British cathedral. It was used by Elizabeth II in 1955; before this however, the last royal visitor to St David's was Edward I in 1284.

There are some particularly fine and fascinating fifteenth century misericords in the choir stalls and the Bishop's Throne – a century younger – has three elaborately pinnacled canopies. The simple shrine to St David himself stands in the north aisle of the choir; his relics, discovered in a rubble-filled recess during mid-nineteenth century restoration work, are contained in an oak casket in the Chapel of the Holy Trinity.

During the seventeenth and eighteenth centuries St David's, despite valiant efforts, decayed. The eminent architect John Nash attempted a restoration at the end of the eighteenth century but the results were surprisingly tasteless. It was left to the great Victorian Sir Gilbert Scott to rectify the error.

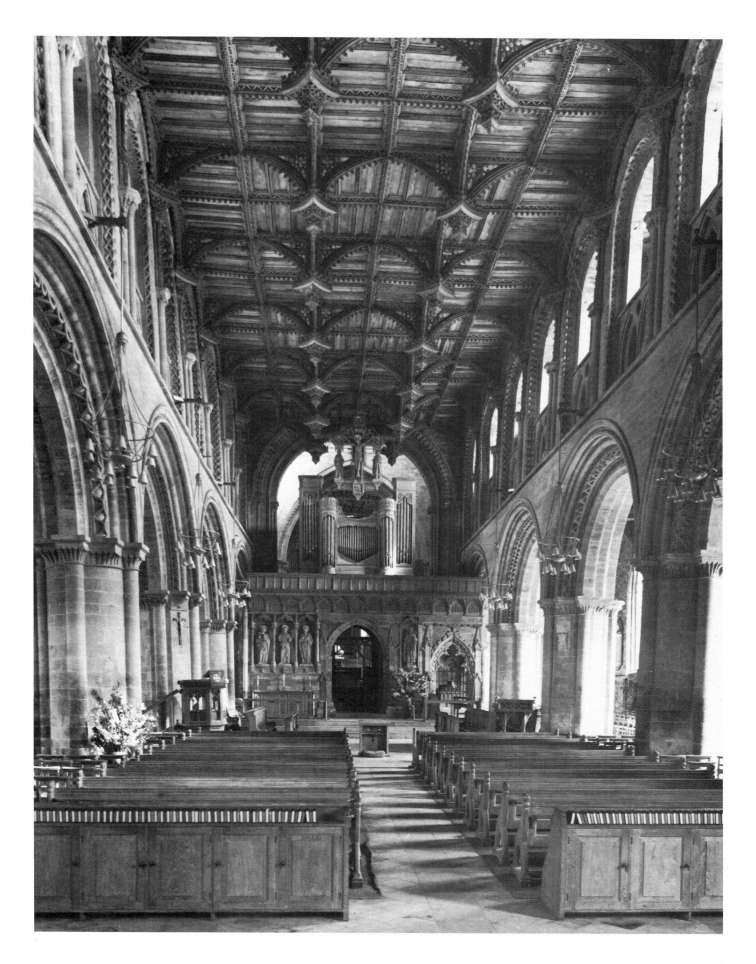

St Paul's

Although the mighty dome of St Paul's Cathedral surmounted by its gold cross has long ago been dwarfed by twentieth century office blocks, it still remains one of London's most famous landmarks and a lasting tribute to the architect, Sir Christopher Wren.

St Paul's stands on the site of four previous cathedrals bearing the same name. The first was built in the seventh century and destroyed by fire; the second was wrecked by the Vikings; the third suffered a fire and the fourth, built by Bishop Maurice, chaplain to William the Conqueror, was destroyed by yet another fire – the Great Fire of London in 1666. All that was left of the medieval cathedral – the largest church in England – was a few columns, part of the walls and a strange shrouded effigy of John Donne, Dean of St Paul's from 1621 until his death in 1631.

Sir Christopher Wren had already been involved in early plans for the restoration of the Norman cathedral. Now he was asked to submit plans for a totally new building. Wren produced three schemes: the first was rejected as untraditional; the second – the magnificent oak model of which can be seen in the trophy room – was turned down for the same reason but eventually the third was grumblingly accepted, with reservations by the Commissioners.

The foundation stone was laid on June 21st 1675 and the cathedral finally completed in 1708. The whole project had been so beset with argument and controversy that it was three years later before Wren received payment in full – and then only after he had personally petitioned Queen Anne. He was dismissed as Surveyor General in 1718 and died in 1723 at the age of ninety one. His body was buried in the crypt – the largest in Europe – and his tomb marked with the

Overleaf: When the soot and grime was cleaned away in the mid-1960s, St Paul's white Portland stone was revealed again after 250 years.

Left: The incomparable west front of St Paul's Cathedral, one of London's most famous and best-loved landmarks.

word's 'Si monumentum requiris, circumspice' – 'If you seek his monument, look round'.

Wren shares the crypt with many of Britain's most illustrious names. Only two, however, the Duke of Wellington and Lord Nelson, are actually interred in their tombs: the others were laid to rest in the ground. These include the painters Holman Hunt, Reynolds, Turner and Millais; Lawrence of Arabia; Florence Nightingale and the composer, Sir Arthur Sullivan. Wellington is also commemorated by a massive monument, which took 20 years to build, situated in the north aisle of the nave.

The stunningly beautiful interior of St Paul's was decorated by some of the world's leading seventeenth and eighteenth century craftsmen; Grinling Gibbons carved the choir stalls; Jean Tijou made the exquisitely complex wrought-iron sanctuary gates while the eight frescoes in the dome were painted by James Thornhill who was knighted in 1720 and appointed serjeant painter to the Crown.

The dome is St Paul's crowning glory, both inside and out. It is 102 feet in diameter and reaches 364 feet into the air at the tip of its cross – just 40 feet lower than the spire at Salisbury. It survived the bombs of the Second World War although the choir roof and the north transept suffered direct hits. Much of the stained glass was so badly damaged during this period that it was later replaced with the clear glass of today. This was what Wren had intended originally and from the way the light enhances the interior, it is easy to see why.

In the mid 1960s St Paul's Portland stone was cleaned. The removal of two and a half centuries of soot and grime revealed once more the quality and soft whitish colour of the cathedral fabric as well as exposing some hitherto barely discernable carving.

Salisbury

As well as being one of England's loveliest cathedrals Salisbury is, architecturally, one of the most important. Built between 1220 and 1284 it is the only example of a medieval cathedral which is wholly consistent in both design and construction. True, its lofty spire – 404 feet high and the tallest in the country – was not added until the mid-fourteenth century, but its tapering delicacy complements perfectly the elegant proportions of the main building below.

Salisbury possesses probably the most attractive setting of Britain's cathedrals. It is approached across the stately eighteenth century lawns of the close, entered through three medieval gates. The close itself, walled in 1333, contains several buildings which pre-date the completion of the cathedral. These include the Bishop's Palace, now the Cathedral School. The most notable of the other later houses is Mompesson House, built by a wealthy merchant family in 1701 and still containing much of the original plasterwork and panelling.

The first cathedral was sited at Old Sarum, a hill-fort town. Five days after it was consecrated in 1092 lightning so severely damaged the structure that it had to be rebuilt. However, it was not long before Bishop Richard Poore, frustrated by lack of a proper water supply, the incessant howling of the wind, the harrassment of his congregations by insensitive soldiers and the continuing complaints of rheumatism by his clergy, petitioned the Pope for permission to erect a new

Below: The nave is 230 feet long and 81 feet high. Everything in it dates from the 13th century.

Right: Salisbury Cathedral viewed across its stately lawns, from the south-west.

cathedral elsewhere. This was duly granted and in 1220, on a well-watered flat site two miles south, work began.

The first section to be finished was the Trinity Chapel at the east end. It was consecrated in 1225 and a plain black stone slab now marks the position of the old shrine of St Osmund, the bishop who completed the first cathedral at Old Sarum. The chapel also contains several tombs, the most notable of which is the imposing monument to the Earl of Hertford and his wife, Lady Jane Grey. A further feature of the chapel, the roof of which is supported by two rows of slender black Purbeck marble columns, is the thirteenth, fourteenth and sixteenth century glass.

By 1258 the nave, transepts and choir were virtually finished and Salisbury was consecrated. The bishop at the time was Giles de Bridport and a handsomely-sculptured tomb – carved with scenes from his life – was later erected for him in the south choir aisle. The cloisters, the largest and earliest of any English cathedral, were completed by 1270, one of their purposes being to provide a passage – the

Right: Salisbury's west front was completed in the mid-13th century. However, many of the larger statues are Victorian additions and do little to enhance the facade.

Plumberies – between the cathedral and the octagonal Chapter House, built between 1263 and 1284. Cromwell's soldiers caused considerable damage to the Chapter House but it was restored in the nineteenth century. Its beautifully fan-vaulted roof rises from a single slender central pillar. The sides are lined with stone seats, above which runs a frieze of thirteenth century stone bas-reliefs depicting Old Testament stories.

There is much to see throughout the cathedral, including many elaborate tombs and monuments. An item of particular fascination is the fourteenth century clock mechanism at the west end of the north aisle. This mechanism – which still works – is believed to be the oldest in Europe. It was installed originally in the old detached bell tower, pulled down in 1790. The fifteenth century library, over the east side of the cloisters, contains many rare and ancient treasures. The most outstanding is one of the four original copies of Magna Carta and a tenth century Gallican Psalter.

Left: The Audley Chantry, built to commemorate Bishop Edward Audley who died in 1524.

Overleaf: The 13th century chapter house with its delicately beautiful fan vault supported by one slender pillar.

Southwark

Towards the end of the nineteenth century Southwark had deteriorated to such an extent that demolition seemed almost inevitable. However, in 1890 London's South Bank cathedral – then a parish church – was reprieved and totally restored. Today, although crowded by other buildings, it remains second only to West-minster in its Gothic glory.

In the days of Edward the Confessor a monastery stood on the site but in 1106 it was reconstructed and 64 years later rededicated to Thomas Becket, follow-ing his untimely death at Canterbury. In the early years of the thirteenth century the church was devastated by a fire. The repairs took nearly 100 years and then, in 1385, there was another fire. Southwark was restored again in the fifteenth century and became a parish church in 1539 when Henry VIII dissolved the monastries. During the eighteenth century decay set in, gradually worsening until the restoration of 1890.

There are still traces of the early building to be found in the interior, even though the nave itself has been completely rebuilt. Sections of thirteenth century arcading can be seen in the south-west corner while at the west end some fine

Right: The tomb of John Gower, Poet Laureate to both Richard II and his successor, Henry IV. Gower, who died in 1408, reclines on three of the books which he wrote.

carved bosses have survived from the fifteenth century wooden roof. An even earlier remnant is a twelfth century door situated in the north aisle which once led to the long disappeared cloisters.

The choir and retro-choir are classic examples of Early English architecture and, generally speaking, Southwark's strongest features; the ornate sixteenth century altar screen is also worth attention. Its Tudor statues have gone but the twentieth century restoration has been sensitively carried out. The aisles of the choir contain several fine tombs including one for James I's 'gentleman porter' John Trehearne and another for Richard Humble, a seventeenth century alderman.

On the east side of the north transept is the Harvard Chapel, dedicated to John Harvard, founder of the famous American university. He was baptized at Southwark in 1607 and emigrated in 1638. The chapel also contains a tablet commemorating the play and song writer, Oscar Hammerstein, who died in 1960.

Southwell Minster

Opposite: Southwell's twin-towered west front.

There is probably no other cathedral in Britain where medieval stone carving reaches such a peak of artistic perfection as it does at Southwell. Nowhere is this more evident than in the chapter house, built at the end of the thirteenth century and Southwell's most celebrated feature.

The entrance to this exquisite octagonal chamber from the vestibule is through a particularly beautiful arched doorway, divided by a slender pillar of extreme delicacy. The equally delicate shafts on each side of the arch provide rare examples of thirteenth century marble. The tops of these shafts and two of the arch mouldings are decorated with stone leaves, intricately and lovingly carved.

Inside the chapter house itself, the most immediately noticeable impression is the lack of a central pillar. This is because the chamber is unusually small – only 31 feet in diameter – and consequently there is no need for an additional support under the magnificent star-vaulted roof. The central boss in the roof is – like every boss on the arched ribs – carved with leaves. The foliage theme predominates: the canopies above each of the 36 stalls and the capitals being decorated with numerous and easily identified foliage, including oak, vine, maple and hawthorn.

Although the chapter house is deservedly the high-point of Southwell's attractions, the cathedral still possesses certain other interesting features. One of these is the fourteenth century stone screen which separates the choir from the nave. This is richly decorated with more than two hundred sculpted heads and figures, including caricatures of the craftsmen actually engaged in its creation. The

Right: The chapter house star vault with its delicately carved rib bosses.

canopies of the attached stalls are carved with the ubiquitous leaves. The brass lectern in the choir, fashioned in the shape of an eagle around 1500 was rescued from a lake where it had been thrown by the monks of nearby Newstead Abbey following the Dissolution. It eventually ended up in the hands of a Nottingham dealer from whom it was bought and presented to Southwell in 1805.

From the north transept, steps lead down into what was once the transept's east wall apse. Since the First World War it has served as the Airmen's Chapel. The altar cross and other fittings were made from the parts of an aircraft which crashed over France.

The origins of Southwell date back to the mid-tenth century when a church was established by Oskytel, Archbishop of York. Hardly anything remains of the Anglo-Saxon building except some pavement fragments in the south transept and a carved tympanum now serving as a lintel over a door in the west wall of the north transept.

The rebuilding of Southwell began during the Norman period with the nave, transepts and west front towers and continued until the end of the thirteenth century. It suffered the indignity of being used as a stable for Parliamentarian horses in the mid-seventeenth century and much of the sculpture and stained glass was smashed beyond repair. Restoration work was carried out in both the eighteenth and nineteenth centuries.

Wells

The west front of Wells Cathedral is a Gothic masterpiece and universally recognized as the most exquisite among Britain's cathedrals. It serves as a screen for an incredible display of statues – once numbering four hundred but now reduced to three hundred – half of which are life-size or larger.

This is undoubtedly the finest collection of medieval statues in the country. Running in six tiers they represent monarchs, prophets, apostles, saints and angels although many have suffered badly from the depredations of age, weather and vandalism. Their bright colours have long since faded but when newly finished by local craftsmen in 1249 they must have seemed one of the wonders of the medieval age.

Wells, often described as our most 'poetic' cathedral, was consecrated in 1239 and the building finally completed in the mid-fifteenth century. The great central tower was raised between 1315 and 1322. This increased the weight so much that sixteen years later cracks started appearing in the masonry and the tower began tilting westwards.

The solution to what could have been a disaster, took the form of ingenious inverted arches designed to transfer the load from west to east; widening the foundations and bracing the tower supports. The arches, inserted around 1338 on three sides – the choir screen providing the necessary support on the fourth – now

Left: The nave, showing one of the three great 'scissor' arches erected under the central tower in 1338 to act as extra support for the newly heightened central tower which, it was feared, might prove too heavy for the foundations.

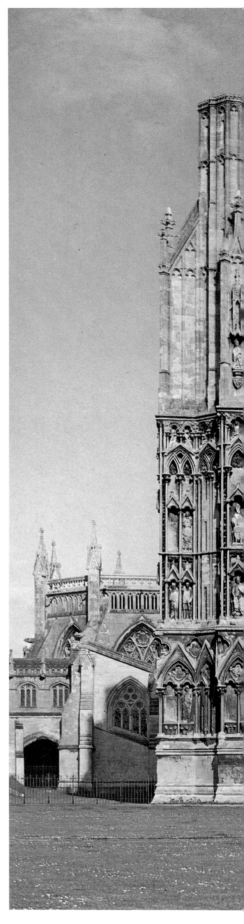

Above: An impressive example of fan vaulting at Wells Cathedral.
Opposite: The west front, one of the most outstanding examples of 13th century architecture still in existence today.
Overleaf: Wells Cathedral contains some very fine stained glass, especially at the east end.

form one of the cathedral's most interesting and striking features. Needless to say the tower has remained solid and upright ever since.

Another feature is the early fourteenth century elevated Chapter House, octagonal in shape and so beautifully decorated that it is surely one of the finest from this period. The worn stairway to the Chapter House was extended to the Chain Gate – a covered way from the cathedral to the Vicar's Hall – in the mid-fifteenth century.

The Lady Chapel, built around the same time, is also a classic example of medieval architecture and craftsmanship at its best. The chapel is linked to the stone-panelled presbytery by a splendidly vaulted retro-choir and possesses five large stained glass windows of which only one is not early fourteenth century, although they have all been patched at later dates. Wells' finest piece of stained glass is the Golden Window inserted in 1340 on the east side of the presbytery.

The cathedral contains the usual tombs of bishops and four fifteenth century chantry chapels of which one, Bishop Beckington's, retains its medieval colouring The Victorian choir stalls incorporate about 60 misericords dating from the early fourteenth century.

Outside the cathedral itself is the moated Bishop's Palace where swans pull a bell rope when they want to be fed and the unique Vicar's Close, two rows of 21 houses built in the mid-fourteenth century.

Westminster Abbey

Strictly speaking, as Westminster Abbey – not to be confused with the neo-Byzantine Roman Catholic cathedral nearby – only enjoyed cathedral status between 1540 and 1550 it has no place in this book. However, its unique situation as Britain's 'royal' church and all the concomitant splendour more than ensures its deserved inclusion.

Westminster was built first by the saintly English king, Edward the Confessor and consecrated on December 28th 1065, a few days before his death. On Christmas Day the following year the victorious William the Conqueror staged his coronation in the abbey. Since then, except for Richard I, Edward V and Edward VIII, every English monarch has been crowned there. On each occasion the ancient coronation chair, made in 1300 to house the Stone of Scone – captured from the Scots in 1296 – is brought out of St Edward's Chapel.

Many of them are also buried at Westminster, sharing their last resting place with great men and women from almost every walk of life: statesmen, authors, poets, musicians, scientists and fighting men. The eighteenth century saw the erection of memorials to eminent people buried elsewhere.

In 1245, less than two hundred years after Edward's great abbey was completed, Henry III pulled it down and started again. He wanted it refashioned in the French style – full of light and gracefully proportioned. In 1268 the remains of the now canonized Edward were brought back to Westminster from their

Below: Henry VII's ornate and elaborate 16th century chapel is probably Westminster's chief glory.

Overleaf: Eleanor of Castille, wife of Edward I, rests in a tomb in St Edward's Chapel. She died in 1290, 17 years before her husband.
Opposite: Westminster Abbey, Britain's royal church, from the west front.

temporary home and enshrined in a tomb of such magnificence that it virtually bankrupted Henry III. Part of it was destroyed in 1540 following the dissolution of the monasteries but later restored during the reign of Mary I. Close by are the tombs of several other kings and queens, including Henry III himself.

Building continued slowly after Henry III's death in 1272 and it was not until the end of the fourteenth century that the abbey was largely complete. Then, in 1503, Henry VII decided he wanted a new Lady Chapel. The next 16 or so years were spent creating Henry VII's Chapel, certainly the chief glory of Westminster and one of the finest of its kind anywhere in the world. Henry VII and his queen lie in a vast Italianate tomb, surrounded by innumerable statues and looked down on by a fan vaulted roof of breathtaking beauty. Close by are the tombs of Mary, Queen of Scots and Elizabeth I while the banners lining the walls belong to the Knights Grand Cross of the Order of the Bath. The chapel has been theirs since 1725.

Those who died anonymously during the First World War are commemorated by a black slab of moving simplicity, the tomb of the Unknown Warrior, set in the floor near the west entrance. Beneath the stone lie the remains of an unknown soldier brought back from France and buried with great pomp on Armistice Day, November 11, 1920. Nearer the west door is another memorial, this time to Sir Winston Churchill, unveiled by the Queen in 1965.

Apart from general restoration and routine maintenance, no major building has occurred since 1734 with the completion of the west front towers. Until then these were only half-built, giving the abbey an unfinished air. They were finally brought to their present height by the architect Nicholas Hawksmoor, using an original design of Sir Christopher Wren.

Above: One of Westminster's treasures, a gilded plate used for the collection of alms or donations for the poor and needy.
Right: A portrait of St Peter, part of a 13th century retable.

Westminster Cathedral

Twelve and a half million bricks went into building Westminster Cathedral, England's leading Roman Catholic church, and it was constructed in the remarkably short time of eight years, from 1895 to 1903.

From outside it is quite unlike any other church, the red bricks alternating with greyish-white limestone in narrow bands to give it an exotic neo-Byzantine air. Its campanile – or bell tower – is square and reaches 284 feet to the top of the cross.

The cathedral interior is truly vast, 342 feet long and 149 feet wide and is laid out in the basilican pattern with four domes in the roof. At the west end are two huge columns made from red Norwegian granite. At the moment the decoration is incomplete but when finished it is intended that the walls and piers will be covered with coloured marble up to a height of 30 feet. Beyond that the walls – and the insides of the domes – will be lined with mosaics.

The side chapels, however, are already richly decorated. One of the most splendid is the Chapel of the Blessed Sacrament on the left of the Sanctuary. Its sumptuous mosaics symbolizing the Trinity and the Blessed Sacrament were fashioned between 1956 and 1962 by Boris Anrep.

Other chapels include the Chapel of St Patrick and the Saints of Ireland. This acts as a memorial to all the Irishmen who died in the First World War, each regiment being commemorated with a marble tablet. Next door is the chapel dedicated to St Andrew and the Saints of Scotland. This is decorated in a typically Byzantine manner and contains a set of impressive choir stalls made from inlaid ebony.

The altar table in the Sanctuary consists of a great block of Cornish granite

Left: The Lady Chapel.

Above: Westminster Cathedral's striking and unusual exterior.

weighing 12 tons. It is flanked with coloured marble arcades while the baldacchino, or canopy, above is made of white marble supported by columns of yellow Verona marble.

An early fifteenth century Madonna in alabaster can be found in the south transept while above on the pier there is an interesting bronze panel by Giacomo Manzu depicting St Teresa of Lisieux.

The crypt under the main body of the cathedral contains several relic chambers. One holds a mitre which once belonged to Thomas Becket, another, fragments of the True Cross.

Winchester

The origins of Winchester Cathedral date back as far as 645 although apart from the mortuary chests containing the bones of various Anglo-Saxon monarchs – including Canute and his wife Emma – nothing now remains from those days when Winchester was the capital of England.

The old cathedral was enlarged in the tenth century but as usual it was the Normans who were responsible for the basis of what stands today. In 1079 Bishop Walkelyn, successor to the last Anglo-Saxon bishop, started building the nave, transepts, choir and chapel, finishing in 1093 when the new cathedral was consecrated. Slightly more than a century later the Norman eastern chapel was pulled down and replaced with a retro-choir and a Lady Chapel, flanked by two other chapels.

This provided a more suitable setting for St Swithin's shrine. Swithin, an earlier bishop, died in 862 leaving instructions that he was to be buried *outside* the old cathedral. When it was decided in 971 to transfer his remains to the interior it is reputed to have rained for forty days. From that day forward the legend has persisted that if it rains on St Swithin's Day – July 15 – it will continue to pour for forty days.

The most significant work on the cathedral was carried out between 1346 and 1404 by Bishops Edington and Wykeham respectively. This involved rebuilding the Norman nave almost stone by stone and linking the Norman choir with the later retro-choir. Since then no further major construction has occurred. However, the cathedral interior has been the centre of extensive and lavish decoration. Winchester now boasts probably the finest collection of chantry chapels in any cathedral. The most ornate of these is dedicated to Cardinal Beaufort, the fifteenth

Below: Winchester Cathedral. Two kings were crowned at Winchester – Edward the Confessor and Richard the Lionheart – when the city was the capital of England.

REVA
RICA
TVS
E
S
T
O
AB

misit: postquam mortuus est achab.
Ceciditq; ochozias prancellos cenaculi
sui quod habebat insamaria. & egrota
uit: misitq; nuntios dicens ad eos. Ite
consulite beelzebub dm accaron: utru
uiuere queam de infirmitate mea hac.
Angelus aute dm locutus est ad helia
thesbiten dicens. Surge ascende in
occursum nuntiorum regis samarie.
& dices ad eos. Numquid non est ds
misrt. ut eatis adconsulendu beelze
bub dm accaron: Quam obrem hec
dicit dns. Delectulo sup que ascen

hec dicit rx. Festina descende. Respon
helias ait. Si homo dei ego sum. descende
de celo. & deuoret te. & quinquaginta
scendit ergo ignis decelo. & deuorauit
quinquaginta eius. Iterum misit prin
quinquagenarium tertium. & quin
qui erant cum eo. Qui cum uenisset
genua contra heliam. & precatus est
homo dei. noli despicere animam m
animam seruorum tuorum qui mecum
descendit ignis decelo. & deuorauit
ipes quinquagenarios primos. & qu
nos qui cum eis erant. sed nunc obse
rearis anime mee. Locutus est aute
ad heliam dicens. Descende cueo. ne
Surrexit igitur & descendit cum eo ad
& locutus est ei. Hec dicit dns. Quia m
tios ad consulendum beelzebub dm a
quasi non eet ds in isrl aquo possis m
sermone: ideo delectulo sup que asc
non descendes. sed morte morieris.
Mortuus est ergo iuxta sermonem dn
uit est helias. & regnauit ioram fr
peo anno sedo ioram filii iosafach reg
enim habebat filium. Reliqua aute u
ochozie que opatus est: nonne hec ser
in libro sermonum dierum regum isrl

century prelate-statesman responsible for Joan of Arc's condemnation.

During the Reformation many of Winchester's treasures were seized and much of the cathedral's interior was despoiled, including St Swithin's shrine. It was eventually restored in 1962. In 1642 Winchester was again subjected to fanatical indignities: Cromwell's soldiers rode their horses up to the altar, kicked it over and then proceeded to destroy systematically as much as they could. The chantries were wrecked; the mortuary chests opened and the bones scattered on the floor and the fine organ pulled down. Since the Restoration a great deal has been done to repair the damage but much – including fourteenth century carvings – was beyond saving.

Winchester is the longest medieval church in Europe – 556 feet – and was used for the coronations of Edward the Confessor and Richard the Lionheart. Among its unique features are the retro-choir which has the most extensive medieval tiled floor in the country and the choir stalls, carved in 1308 – the oldest still in existence, likewise the wrought iron gates in the south transept.

Among the other numerous features are a twelfth century font made from black Tournai marble; a stone marking the burial place of Jane Austen; a stained glass window commemorating Izaak Walton; the mortuary chests set on the choir screens and – the cathedral's most valuable possession – an illuminated twelfth century Bible, written in Latin.

Opposite: One of the illuminated pages from the 12th century Winchester Bible, the cathedral's most treasured and valuable possession.
Opposite below: The twelve-bay nave, the largest of its kind in the world, and a detail from the 12th century font made from black Tournai marble.

STUDY TO BE QUIET

Above: The Isaak Walton memorial window in Prior Thomas Silkestede's chapel. Walton, best remembered for his book the Compleat Angler, died in 1683 and was buried in the chapel.
Left: This shrine to St Swithin was donated to the cathedral in 1962. The original shrine had been destroyed by Henry VIII's commissioners in 1538.

Worcester

King John was a frequent visitor to Worcester and when he realized he was dying – from dysentry aggravated by over indulging in peaches and new cider – he asked to be buried in the church.

On October 18 1216 he died. His body was brought from Newark and laid in a plain stone coffin in front of the high altar. The Purbeck marble effigy – added sixteen years later – shows John lying between two much smaller figures. They are believed to be the Saints Oswald and Wulstan, two of Worcester's earliest bishops. The lion biting the king's sword tip symbolizes the baron's curbing of royal power with Magna Carta the year before his death. In 1529 a richly decorated tomb was erected around the coffin.

Prince Arthur, eldest son of Henry VII, is also buried at Worcester. He died at Ludlow Castle at the age of 15 and was entombed at Worcester after a lavish funeral on April 25 1502. Two years later a magnificent pinnacled chantry was built to house the tomb. It stands to the south of the high altar, just a short distance from the tomb of King John.

The cathedral itself, serenely situated on the east banks of the River Severn, dates back as far as 680 when Bosel, a priest from Whitby in Yorkshire, was consecrated as the first Bishop of Worcester. Around 983 Oswald, who served both Worcester and York as archbishop until his death, founded a Benedictine monastery on the site of the present nave. Towards the mid-eleventh century a young priest called Wulstan was admitted to the monastery. In 1062 he was appointed bishop and became the only Anglo-Saxon incumbent of such office to hold his position for any length beyond the Conquest. Wulstan in fact helped officiate at William's coronation in Westminster.

Once he was firmly established, Wulstan began an extensive building programme. Worcester was in a fairly delapidated state, having been sacked by the Danes in 1041 and left to moulder quietly ever since. One of his first tasks was the crypt and much of this still remains – the largest of its kind in England – its stout plain Norman pillars dividing the shadowy aisles.

Wulstan died in 1095 and was canonized in 1203 after various miracles had been attributed to him. This attracted pilgrims which in turn swelled the coffers. More building started, resulting in a remodelling of the choir and the construction of the richly decorated Lady Chapel. Much of its original charm and beauty survives although the stained glass and ceiling work belong to the nineteenth century.

Early in the fourteenth century it was decided to rebuild the nave and bring it more in line with the style of the cathedral's east end – itself remodelled to match the delicacy of the Lady Chapel. Work continued towards the end of the century and then stopped – for no apparent reason – along the north side of the nave. This preserved – fortunately – one of Worcester's most interesting architectural features: the twelfth century transitional Norman arches with their elaborate ornamented triforium – the upper part of the wall. As is clearly seen they differ completely from all the others.

Worcester's finest external feature is the stately fourteenth century central tower, built to replace its Norman predecessor which collapsed in 1175.

Overleaf: Looking east along the nave of Worcester Cathedral towards the High Altar.

Right: A romantic view of Worcester Cathedral, set picturesquely on the eastern banks of the River Severn.

York Minster

York is not only the largest medieval cathedral in northern Europe but it also boasts more original stained glass than any other comparable church. This includes the magnificent Old Testament east window behind the high altar, a breathtaking 78 feet by 31 feet, one of the world's biggest sheets of medieval glazing.

The cathedral was built between 1220 and 1470, two and a half centuries of dedicated craftsmanship that has resulted in a medieval masterpiece. Although restored and refurbished several times since the fifteenth century – the last major work taking place as recently as the late 1960s – York still stands firm and proud, a perpetual monument to the skill of its builders.

A simple wooden chapel once stood on the site now occupied by York. It was built for the baptism of Edwin, King of Northumbria in 627. This was replaced by a stone church which lasted until 741 when it was burnt down. The ravages of the Norman Conquest put paid to the next church. There was some desultory building during the eleventh and twelfth centuries but it was not until Walter de

Below: The massive bulk of York's east end, often compared with a sheer cliff face.

Gray became Archbishop in 1216 that the cathedral in its present form began to take shape.

De Gray, an influential figure in the Government of Henry III, is now housed in a splendid tomb on the east side of the south transept. He is one of about a dozen archbishops buried in the cathedral. They include Richard Scrope who was beheaded in 1405 after taking part in an unsuccessful uprising against Henry IV. Soon after his death miracles were attributed to him and he was eventually canonized. His somewhat plain tomb is situated in the Lady Chapel opposite the infinitely more ornate one erected to Archbishop Bowet who died in 1423.

Another tomb of particular interest is that of Prince William of Hatfield, a younger son of Edward III. It is surmounted with an effigy of the youth, his feet resting against a crouching lion, in the north aisle of the choir.

Edward himself was married at York in January 1328 at the age of 15. Later, when he was embroiled in the Scottish wars, Edward governed England from York. The Chapter House was used by the royal chancery and baronial shields along the nave walls date from this period. The Chapter House was restored in the mid-nineteenth century but still retains much of its original grace. There is no central column supporting its immense fourteenth century painted roof, an admirable feat of medieval engineering.

York possesses many unique and fascinating architectural features but its greatest treasure is the incredible expanse of incomparable stained glass: the east window already mentioned; a soaring fourteenth century west window depicting New Testament scenes, apostles and archbishops; the Five Sisters window from 1250 in the north transept and, what is believed to be the oldest piece of stained glass in the world – a twelfth century panel in the north aisle of the nave.

Right: The south choir aisle.

Below: The 14th century Zouche Chapel.

Picture credits

Barnaby's Picture Library 26; British Museum 5L; British Tourst Authority 15L; 20; 22; 29TR & BR; 31; 34; 35; 36R; 39; 40; 41; 49; 82; 105; 117; 120BL; 121R; Colour Library International 8/9; 28; 56; 72/3; 80; 81; 83; 84; 88; 90; 118; 124; 126; Conway Picture Library 70BL; Department of the Environment for Northern Ireland 7; J. Arthur Dixon 63; C. M. Dixon 58; Derek Evans FRPS, FRSA. 50; John Freeman 12/13; Ray Green 66T; Sonia Halliday 46; 54; 57; 71; 127; Michael Holford 11; 12T; 15R; 17; 18; 38; 42/3; 47; 55; 68; 70TR; 76/7; 78, 85; 98; 111; 115; 116; Angelo Hornak 96; 100; 102/3; Jarrold & Son, Norwich 69; Judges Ltd. 121L; A. F. Kersting 3T; 21; 23; 24/5; 32; 33; 36/7; 45; 48; 53; 61; 62; 74; 75; 76; 89; 93; 98/9; 114L & R; 123; 125; Keystone Press 79; Brian Gentry Long 8; 10; T. C. Leaman 112; Manchester Evening News & Guardian 65; National Monuments Record 59; 60; 86L; 104; National Monuments Record in Wales 87; 92; National Trust 101; Northern Ireland Tourist Board 6; 64; Picturepoint 14; 16/17; 44; 109; 113; 128; Pitkin Pictorial Ltd./photos Sydney Newbery 19; 51; 52; 66BL & BR; 67; 86R; 91; 106; 108; Saxon Artists 2; 3R; Bruce Scott 12B; 36L; Kenneth Scowan 94/5; 119; Shepherd Building Group 5R; Brian Shuel 27; 29L; 30; 110; E. Sollars 120T; E. W. Tattershall 107; Richard Tilbrook/'The Light of the World' by William Holman Hunt 97; Transworld Feature Syndicate 120BR; Ziolo 4; Interiors reproduced by courtesy of the Dean and Chapter of St. Patrick's Cathedral, Armagh; Bristol Cathedral; Canterbury Cathedral; Chester Cathedral; Chichester Cathedral; Coventry Cathedral; Durham Cathedral; Ely Cathedral; Exeter Cathedral; Gloucester Cathedral; Hereford Cathedral; Lichfield Cathedral; Lincoln Cathedral; Anglican Cathedral, Liverpool; Llandaff Cathedral; St. Columb's Cathedral, Londonderry; Manchester Cathedral; Norwich Cathedral; Christchurch, Oxford; Peterborough Cathedral; Ripon Cathedral; Rochester Cathedral; St. Alban's Cathedral; St. Asaph's Cathedral; St. David's Cathedral; St. Paul's Cathedral; Salisbury Cathedral; Southwark Cathedral; Southwell Cathedral; Wells Cathedral; Westminster Abbey; Winchester Cathedral; Worcester Cathedral; York Minster; St. Giles.